READY FOR BATTLE!

Training Kingdom Warriors to Tear Down the Kingdom of Darkness

READY FOR BATTLE!

Training Kingdom Warriors to Tear Down the Kingdom of Darkness

DR. WANDA COFIELD

READY FOR BATTLE!

TRAINING KINGDOM WARRIORS TO TEAR DOWN THE KINGDOM OF DARKNESS!

ISBN: 978-1-945456-11-4

Printed in the United States of America.

Cover Design:
Mark Oberkrom

Editor:
Letrecia Myers

TABLE OF CONTENTS

Dedications

First and foremost, I like to thank My Heavenly Father, for without God and His love for me I do not know where I would be. I am forever grateful for His Love, grace and mercy.

To my loving and devoted husband George, thank you for being my biggest supporter and pushing me when I didn't want to push anymore. You have been a constant encourager throughout this process. You truly are an awesome gift from God! Love you for life! #TeamCofields

My children, Alicia, Georgia and Wallace. You all are a gift from God that I cherish and love dearly. You all are destined for Greatness and your latter shall be GREATER! Thank you all for your love and support!

To my Pastors, Robert and Alicia Dowell, words cannot express how much I appreciate you both and the push to go further and seeing things in me that I didn't see. I am forever grateful to you both!

A special dedication to my grandson, Leonard Battle III. You were only here on this earth for two months, but I found out going through this made me stronger and this ordeal helped me PUSH THIS BOOK OUT! I will love you forever LB3!

To all of my supporters, I thank you from the bottom of my heart. I appreciate you all, and I am forever grateful.

Foreword

"Ready for Battle" by Dr. Wanda Cofield is a must read for every believer. In these last and evil days, we are facing new threats and challenges in our world, churches, and individual lives. It is indeed time to get *"Ready for Battle"*. Ephesians 6:12 declares, *"For we wrestle not against flesh and blood, but against principalities, against powers, against the rulers of the darkness of this world, against spiritual wickedness in high places."* In this scripture, we discover that our battle is a spiritual battle and not a physical one. Therefore, it is essential that we have spiritual tools like this book to be successful in our spiritual battle. Not only does Dr. Cofield challenge you to answer the call as a Kingdom Warrior, but she also gives guidance and direction to help equip you as a Kingdom Warrior. She does a masterful job in teaching believers how to put their war clothes on. As you read this book, you will receive an anointing to cause you to move from worrier to warrior. After reading, you will have a fight mentality and not a flight mentality. As you feast on this powerful and insightful teaching and training, you will experience a fresh wind that will empower you to win. You will be strengthened to bounce back from your last attack. The Spirit of the Lord will empower you in areas where the enemy was trying to devour you.

We as believers must never forget that we are not on this earth by accident, or by coincident. We are here by divine providence. We all have a divine mission to fulfill. To carry out our mission, we must be in the right position. This book will give you the revelation and motivation you need to get in the proper position. We are in the right place when we are armed, trained and *"Ready for Battle"*. This season is not a time for believers to sit back or step back. It is time to stand up and step up. It is time to get in position. It is time to get *"Ready for Battle"!*

Dr. Robert F. Dowell
Senior Pastor,
New Life Fellowship
Lawton, OK

INTRODUCTION

Just what is the Kingdom of Darkness and how can it be torn down? The Kingdom of Darkness is a kingdom of spiritual lies and deception. It is operated by hatred, fear, control and competition for power. Imagine you are out at night on a tiny boat in a body of water. Darkness surrounds you, with no hint of light in sight. Rowing the boat, you wonder if you are even going in the right direction. Everywhere you turn to look is gloom. And because it is so obscure, you can't see what's in front of you, beside you, or behind you. Falling prey to the unknown, your mind starts to play tricks on you by saying, "if you get out of this boat, something is going to destroy you." This is the place where the Enemy wants us--where we cannot see where we are going and where we become fearful of the unknown.

For we wrestle not against flesh and blood, but against principalities, against powers, against the rulers of the darkness of this age, against spiritual hosts of wickedness in the heavenly places.

Ephesians 6:12

Warriors when you are fighting for God, you are filled with the Holy Spirit and everywhere you go you bring light. So when we enter to a place where it is dark, light immediately turns on. There is no power in darkness. When you think about your home, you need power to have lights. We typically have power from electricity. If you do not pay your electricity bill, you will not have any power. As vessels to be used by God, we have been given the power and tools to keep our lights on. As warriors, we should never be afraid of the darkness because it is powerless. Darkness is afraid of us because of the power that dwells inside of us. It's time to let your light shine, warriors. Now is the time Warriors to get trained to tear down the Kingdom of Darkness! This book will equip you with the tools and training you need to tear down the Kingdom of Darkness brick by brick. Are you READY WARRIOR!

Prayer

Father God, thank You for choosing me to train as Your warrior to tear down the Kingdom of Darkness. Thank You for giving me an ear to hear Your voice and the sound of the trumpet. The walls are coming down as I prepare for battle. I stand with an open heart and a spirit of expectancy. I stand with a yielded heart to learn from You. I am trusting in You Lord to prepare me for battle. I say YES Lord. Amen.

Chapter One

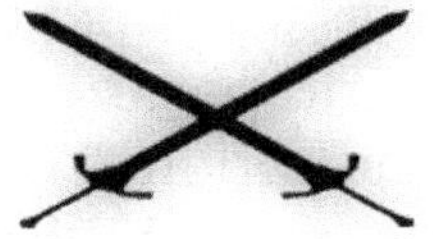

TIME TO PREPARE AND ACCEPT THE CALLING OF A WARRIOR

The definition of prepare is to make something ready for use or consideration. God wants to get us ready for what is to come. He wants us trained and ready in all areas of our lives. If we are not prepared, we cannot be considered ready for His use. Warriors our desire should always want to be considered to be used by the Father. In our time of preparing we are learning things about ourselves. We are learning our bad habits; we are learning our strengths, and weaknesses. The time of preparation is not a pretty place because we are in deep training. I remember when I was in the Army and I had to go to Air Assault school and we had to wear a ruck sack that weighed around 20 pounds and we had to complete a 12 mile road march in under 3 hours as one of the criteria's to graduate. The first 6 mile road march I failed. I could not complete it under an hour and a half so I knew, I had to prepare because I knew I was not ready for this 12 mile road march in the allotted time. I had to march with a ruck sack and boots on my own. I had to PREPARE for the upcoming road march. This was my time of preparation so that I could be ready for use for graduation. This makes me think about the 10 virgins in the bible.

Then shall the kingdom of heaven be likened unto ten virgins, which took their lamps, and went forth to meet the bridegroom. And five of them were wise, and five were foolish. They that were foolish took their lamps, and took no oil with them; But the wise took oil in their vessels with their lamps. While the bridegroom tarried, they all slumbered and slept. And at midnight there was a cry made, Behold, the bridegroom cometh; go ye out to meet him. Then all those virgins arose, and trimmed their lamps. And the foolish said unto the wise, Give us of your oil; for our lamps are gone out. But the wise answered, saying, Not so; lest there be not enough for us and you: but go ye rather to them that sell, and buy for yourselves. And while they went to buy, the bridegroom came; and they that were ready went in with him to the marriage: and the door was shut. Afterward came also the other virgins, saying, Lord, Lord, open to us. But he answered and said, Verily I say unto you, I know you not. "

Matthew 25:1-12

This is a great illustration of preparing to be ready for use and how when you do not properly prepare, you will not be considered for the Master's Use. Five of the virgins prepared and had oil in their lamps and the other five did not properly prepare. When you prepare yourself you are positioning and aligning yourself for great blessings. What better blessing than to be prepared for the use of the King of Kings. Warriors, what are you doing for your time of preparation? Are you serious about your preparation time? Preparation time for ministry is not just about us, but it is also about others.

We need to understand that the ministry God placed in us is just not about ministering to ourselves. It is a must to know that others' souls are at stake. As warriors, God has called us to tear up and tear down things in the spirit that have our brothers and sisters in dark places. God has called us to go tear down the walls around the people of God through that ministry, and in order for us to tear down the Kingdom of Darkness, we need training. In order for us to do this, we have to launch missiles with God's anointing. We have to stay ready for attack and be prepared for battle at any given time.

When you accept the calling of a warrior you have accepted the mission that it is not just about your local church but it is Kingdom Work and tearing down the Kingdom of Darkness!

You have to know who you are. You are not just a minister who is a warrior--you are a Kingdom Warrior who God has called to go and tear down the barriers of the Enemy. God wants you to be the warrior that He has designed you to be. A Kingdom Warrior is a person of faith who says, "This is what I love to do, and this is what I am called to do." True Kingdom Warriors, war for their family, they war for what God believes in and they war for what

God stands for. A warrior does not want the Enemy to cause a threat to any of these things and they stand their ground and remain watchmen on the wall. A warrior tells the Enemy "You cannot have my family. You cannot have my children. You cannot have the ministry God birthed in me. You cannot have my sister or brother in Christ without coming through me."

- ❖ A Kingdom Warrior is not afraid to fight because they know that God is with them

- ❖ A Kingdom Warrior does not operate under his/her flesh but operates under the unction of the Holy Spirit.

- ❖ A Kingdom Warrior does not look for man's approval because they know it is not about man, but it is about doing Kingdom work and pleasing the Father.

When you are preparing and training to be a kingdom warrior, you have to literally offer yourself to God -- meaning you have to let the Creator shape and mold you. It does not matter to what area of ministry you are called. We all need to be shaped and molded. You must be willing to be put on the Potter's wheel, so God can get you ready for your assignment. You have to yield to the Holy Spirit. Our God is a gentleman so He will not force you to yield or submit to Him. Being a warrior for Christ is not an easy task. You will be subject to spiritual warfare, and that is why being trained and developed in your area of ministry will help you move forward in victory and not retreat in defeat. During this time of training, you will learn the importance of having things that have been a hindrance to you and to the mission removed from you. Pride, jealousy, disloyalty, division, and fear are just some of the things that will need to be taken off of us. How can we tear down the Kingdom of Darkness if we go into battle with issues like low self-esteem, depression, pride, jealousy, fear, and oppression? How can we go into battle if we are not physically fit and we are mentally drained? That is why we must be free from all the distractions before we can go to war. God needs us to be focused before we prepare to minister. When you are preparing to minister and tear down strongholds, you **MUST** have a **spirit of boldness**. You cannot go anywhere to tear down anything without boldness and having a spirit of fear.

"God has not given us the spirit of fear."

2 Timothy 1:7a

We cannot go into battle to tear down the walls of darkness being timid. 'Timid' is an adjective which describes a person who has a lack of courage or confidence and is easily frightened. Those are not characteristics of a kingdom warrior. So, therefore being timid is not who you were called to be in this battle. You have to have a spirit of **boldness** in this war. **Boldness matters! Boldness** is the willingness to do the right thing at the right time regardless of how the situation may look. With the spirit of **boldness,** it enables us to speak the truth and perform our mission without being fearful because we are following God. When we are operating in the spirit of **boldness** we know that God is in control and we do not need to fear what others will do or say because God is with us. **Boldness** comes with the confidence we have in Christ, who He is, and what He can do. **Boldness** is not an arrogant attitude or an aggressive spirit, but it is gentle with courage because we do not stand on our own. We need **boldness** warriors. Without **boldness**, we cannot fulfill God's purpose in our lives and if we cannot fulfill the purpose in our own lives, we definitely are not tearing down any walls of darkness.

When you have accepted the call, there are all kinds of questions that may come up in your mind, like.... "Am I qualified???" "Do I have the ability to do it?" "Are you sure I am the one, Lord?" But the first step is just saying 'yes' and being willing. God will do the rest. So today you have started the journey of accepting the call of the Warrior and you are now ready to ***PREPARE FOR BATTLE!***

Discussion/Self Check

1. What is your mission as a warrior?

____

____

____

____

TIME TO PREPARE AND ACCEPT THE CALLING OF A WARRIOR

2. Have you accepted the call? _________ If not, why? ______________________________________

____

____

____

3. What type of spirit should you have when you are ministering to tear down the spirit of darkness?

____

4. How are you preparing in your training time?

____

____

____

____

Prayer

Father God, help me to realize that I am qualified in You. I say YES to the mission, I say YES to Your will. I will be the Soldier that is Ready For BATTLE! I know that if I put all my trust in You, You shall direct my path. So Father today is the day I come forth. Today, I submit to You. I thank You for giving me the spirit of **BOLDNESS** to tear down the Kingdom of Darkness. Lord, help me to prepare for training so that I am ready for use for You. It is so, and so it shall be, in Jesus Name!

Chapter Two

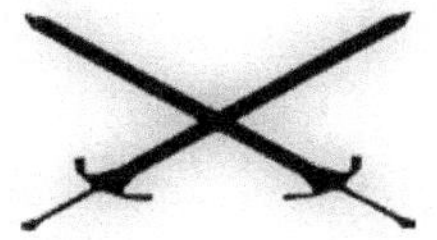

UNDERSTANDING THE MISSION

As Kingdom Warriors, God strategically equips us with movements of mass destruction to tear down the Kingdom of Darkness. ***The song, the instruments, the flags, the hand movements, the march, the prayer, the sermon, ...it's all given to us by God. We are snipers in the prophetic realm of the spirit. We are snipers when we minister!*** A sniper is a qualified specialist who maintains a close visual with the enemy and engages targets from concealed positions or distances without being detected by the enemy. The enemy does not have any idea how and when we are coming and that is because God has positioned us in a place within that we are protected and hidden in Him. God has placed a hedge of protection around us as we minister so the Enemy cannot touch us! God allows us to give the Enemy a double blow to his head and trample over him with our feet with His guidance. Hallelujah! That is something that should get you excited that our Heavenly Father cares about us and loves us so much that He does not send us into war without any protection. I will never minister in dance or preach the word of God thinking I am going to tear down the Kingdom of Darkness without my Father's protection; nor should you. As a warrior in training, you will go through some experiences that will cause you to come out of your comfort zone. It will cause you to do things that at first may seem uncomfortable because you have not always done these things. This training will push you, strengthen you, and encourage you. It will take blinders off your eyes, and it will help you to see things from a different perspective. Although, you may think that you do not have what it takes to complete this training, I am telling you not to throw in the towel because the Trainer you have, has an outstanding record. He has never lost any battles, and you can be rest assured that He is there with you every step you take. You have a great Trainer and Leader that will never leave you nor forsake you in this training or while you are on the battlefield. Your Trainer is a Great Comforter, He is the Great I am, and He is a great Friend. He knows everything about you already, so there is no need to hide anything from Him. He knew you before you were formed in your mother's womb. God is your personal trainer. You can always count on your Trainer to equip you with everything that you will need to lead to you to complete success. This training is designed to train you up as a kingdom warrior that will tear down the Kingdom of Darkness.

This training will:

- ❖ Guide you and keep you all the days of your life.
- ❖ Give you direction.
- ❖ Equip you to rescue others and war on the behalf of others.

You were designed for this, Warrior!

Before we move into any training, it is important to understand the mission. You have to understand why you do what you do in order to grasp the training. Why is there a need for kingdom warriors? Why is training important? If you do not understand the mission, then you will not comprehend the importance of the mission. If you do not understand the "why" of a thing, it can lead you to confusion, frustration, and disappointment and cause you to doubt the very thing God called you to. And when you doubt, it will cause you to have a quitting spirit before you even get started. As a warrior you will go through things that can maybe question if you are really made for this battle. But I am here to tell you, that you are the apple of His eye. You are created for every storm and trial that come your way. You are a survivor, and you are a Kingdom Warrior.

Knowing that you are called is one thing but the "why" is important. Your enemy knows that you are called and the Enemy knows *why* you are called, but he doesn't want you to know *why* you are called. God tells us to get wisdom and in that wisdom get an understanding. Understand that God has a plan for your life. This plan was made before you were born. Understand that all His promises concerning you, are yes and amen. Meaning they are going to come to pass and because you understand the "why", you will better understand your mission.

God needs Kingdom Warriors to move on His behalf. As warriors, our mission is to tear down, block and pull down strongholds. Our mission is to lead others to freedom and help them build a stronger relationship with the Father. We are to preach the gospel of Jesus Christ; we are to bring Jesus to the world. When we preach to the people, we will unfold Satan's plan and let them know that Satan is here to steal, kill and destroy, but God gives life and life more abundantly. Our mission is not something to take lightly, and before we go to others, we must first catch the vision and understand the mission that God has given us.

As Warriors, we have to keep the main thing the main thing, and that is seeking God's face daily, laying in His presence, and living by the Word of God. We are not good to anyone if our primary focus is not seeking God daily through prayer, meditating on the Word, and spending time with our Father. We cannot operate on fumes if we expect to tear down the Kingdom of Darkness. We have to make sure that we are recharging our spirit man daily. We have to realize that the devil has a plan for us, and it is not meant for any good. So when we minister, we need to be ready to tear down the Kingdom of Darkness because we know that the Enemy wants to kill us, our families, and our sisters and brothers in Christ. He has no mercy; he does not know what mercy is. His aim is to attack us and always do evil towards us every day of our lives that we are serving the Lord. This is why we need to minister with a purpose in our heart and that sole purpose is to tear apart the Enemy's camp, help rescue and save the lost souls, and bring them to Jesus. The devil has no mercy for us, so why should we show him or his legions of demons mercy? It is Time to War, Warrior! But you must continue to train in battle if God is going to use you for this purpose. You must eat and maintain a proper spiritual diet if you are going to be able to stand against the wiles of the Enemy. You should be prepared and understand that when God uses you to tear down the Kingdom of Darkness through the ministry in you, the devil is not happy. He is quite upset with you, and just in case you didn't know it, you now have his undivided attention. Because of this, you have to pray for God's strength. We have to be mighty and strong intercessors to be able to minister and do damage to the Enemy's camp. As you are warring, something is happening in the spirit realm. Walls are coming down. There is a battle going on while you are ministering. When you are ministering in dance, in prayer, or in a song you are literally going to "war" with the Enemy, with the intent to cast down the demonic powers in heavenly places. The enemy is coming against Kingdom Warriors. He's seeking us, attacking us and wants to harm us and even destroy us. There is only one thing we and the enemy have in common and that is, we both want to destroy each other. We don't like him and he does not like us. So when we are warring, we need to pray that God moves upon us like never before; like a fresh wind and with a power that will tear down Satan's camp. People's souls are at stake, and our hearts should cry out for the people of God who are trapped and locked behind these walls. Our desire is for them to be free so they can walk out their destiny and purpose. We need them to come out of darkness because they don't realize that they have much work to do for the Kingdom of God. They are

MIA (missing in action), and we need them in place. Their role is important.

The mission at hand is very important, and that is why we need training. Warriors we need to minister before the Lord like never before because our sisters and brothers in Christ are trapped in the Kingdom of Darkness they are POW's (Prisoners of War), and we need to get trained up so we can go and free them. We need to get them home! They need a Kingdom Warrior to set them free. They need a Kingdom Warrior to show them the light because they have been living in darkness for way too long. Are you that one warrior? Do you understand the mission?

Some people look at us and say "They don't have any power to release anything or do any damage to the Kingdom of Darkness", and they are right. Warriors, in their own power, cannot do a thing, but when God touches it and blows His fresh anointing on it; that's when it tears down the Kingdom of Darkness and that gives me joy and that is one reason why I minister. It brings great joy to me when I see my brothers and sisters set free. That's the blessing and that is why we are called to do what we do. That is why we have to understand the importance of our mission. We have to know that we are Ambassadors for Christ. We have been given the power of the Holy Spirit, and we have a legal right as Kingdom citizens to go to the enemy's camp, take back what he has stolen, and tear his walls down to dust.

God has given me a spirit of boldness, and that is how I minister... with a spirit of **boldness**, and with that **boldness** it tears down the Kingdom of Darkness. The violent take it by force. My dance is a warfare dance. God has given me a spirit of boldness to preach His word, letting the enemy know that God is with me. It is through God's strength and might that I am pulling God's people out of the pit of the enemy. It tears down the walls of the prison (the Kingdom of Darkness) that have been built up around me and my sisters and brothers in Christ.

"About midnight Paul and Silas were praying and singing hymns to God, and the other prisoners were listening to them. Suddenly there was such a violent earthquake that the foundations of the prison were shaken. At once all the prison doors flew open, and everyone's chains came loose".

Acts 16:25-26

Can you imagine right before you get ready to minister, God shows you all the walls that are built up around the people of God? He shows you how many are stuck and trapped in the Kingdom of Darkness. He shows you how many people are crying out, wanting their freedom but don't know how to get it. They need help.

Can you just imagine for a second.............. Now for them, it is a midnight hour. They are frustrated, and they are tired. They feel like giving up and they feel like all hope is lost! But for you, it is the hour of **POWER**, so you smile, knowing that God has called *you,* His sniper. You begin to minister and something starts to happen. God Shows up! As you continue to minister, brick by brick is being destroyed. God is using *you* to render the Kingdom of Darkness **POWERLESS!** It is the anointing of God that is destroying every yolk, every barrier, and every wall. *Can you really grasp your mind around that?*

God wants to use **YOU** to tear down the Kingdom of Darkness, Warrior. I don't know about you, but it took me some time to really grasp that concept. I'm not a big person, but once I caught that revelation, I realized I am HUGE in the spirit because my God dwells inside of me,

"because Greater is He that lives inside of me than he that lives in the world!"

1 John 4:4b

And because God is not a respecter of persons, you are also HUGE in the Spirit, He will use you as well. As you begin to minister you release a praise, and that is a major weapon against the Kingdom of Darkness. *"Perfect Praise Silences the enemy"*

Psalm 8:2

so as you minister, you are tearing down the Kingdom of Darkness by putting a muzzle over the Enemy's mouth. As you begin to minister led by God's Holy Spirit will silence the Enemy and tears down the Kingdom of Darkness....

"It is God who arms me with strength and makes my way perfect. He makes my feet like the feet of a deer; he enables me to stand on the heights. He trains my hands for battle; my arms can bend a bow of bronze. You give me your shield of victory, and your right hand sustains me; you stoop down to make me great. You broaden the path beneath me, so that my ankles do not turn. I pursued my enemies and overtook them; I did not turn back til they were destroyed."

Psalm 18:32-37

Warrior, I understand that this mission is a lot to handle or take on, but remember you have a great Trainer to guide you. Now that you understand your mission, it is time to see how you were designed and created to be used in this battle.

Discussion/Self Check

1. How do you see yourself as a sniper in the Kingdom? ________________________________

____

____

____

2. What is the mission of a Kingdom Warrior?

____

____

____

____

____

Prayer

God, only You can strategically give me what I need in this battle. I turn to You and seek Your face continually. My ears are pressed against Your lips and I will follow only Your voice. Help me to understand the mission and what is needed of me. I thank You for wisdom and for giving me understanding as I prepare for battle. Lord as I lean to You for understanding. I pray that You will continue to equip me for what is needed to get through this training. Thank You, Lord for encouraging me, strengthen me and preparing me for this battle. Amen.

Chapter Three

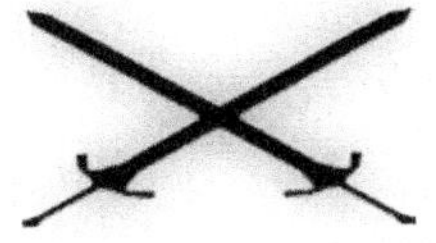

KNOWING WHAT'S INSIDE OF YOU!

As a kingdom warrior in training, you have to know what's inside of you that God wants you to use. Many of us may have different things inside of us that God wants us to use, so it is very important to seek God and let Him reveal to you what He wants to use. Warriors, sometimes we are surrounded by so many people: family, friends, co-workers, and even complete strangers. Oftentimes, many of these people fill our ears with everything *but* what God's wants us to hear concerning us and what is inside of us. As part of your training, you will need to lay before God and be still. He will speak to you, and you have to make sure what others tell you actually agree with your spirit man as well as falls in line with what God has shared with you. Warrior, please understand that God has created you to fulfill a specific role and you are the only one that can achieve what God has purposed you for. That is why you need to know what "it" is inside of you.

"As every man hath received the gift, even so minister the same one to another, as good stewards of the manifold grace of God".

1 Peter 4:10

Meaning that God has gifted every one of us with the "it" for this war. But in order to know what that "it" is inside of you. You first need to know who you are. Many people do not have any idea who they are in Christ. Warriors you cannot have an identity crisis. You can never lose who you are in Christ. Your identity defines your purpose in life. Your identity helps you find what's inside of you. And in order to keep moving forward, you must know what that "it" is that is inside of you. Know who you are in Christ.

Since I have been ministering in dance for the Lord, I understand that my dance is a warfare dance. When I minister in dance, God gives me spiritual movements of warfare. It is a bold dance, full of confidence and faith which demonstrates fighting the battle. When in war mode, as I am ministering in dance and while tearing down the Kingdom of Darkness, I notice that I frequently use my hands. I clap my hands at any given time. It is not practiced, nor do I realize that I am even doing it. So I begin to ask, "Why do I clap my hands when I dance Lord"? He replied, "*I train your hands to war and your fingers to battle*" {**Psalm 144:1**}. He teaches/trains my hands to war, just by ministering in dance. As I am clapping my hands when God instructs me to do so, I am using the detonator to let the explosives go off in the Enemy's camp. My hands are setting off deadly explosives,

CLAP, walls of depression coming down!

CLAP, webs of self-pity coming down!
CLAP, webs of deceit are coming down!
CLAP, no more darkness, but now I can begin to see the light!

I share this with you simply to illustrate how I realize what God has placed inside of me. Not only do I recognize what is inside of me, I understand that God equipped me with this particular tool to use in battle.

Now ask yourself, "What's inside of me Lord, that You have chosen for me to use as a warrior in this WAR?" Whatever that "it" is, you have to learn to perfect it. You have to learn how to operate it so it can be effective. Warrior, I bet you never thought that what is inside of you can bring recovering sight to the blind and preach deliverance to the captives. Knowing what is inside of you is important because it brings healing and restoration. People are in a season now where they have a strong hunger and desire to be free. As warriors, God has anointed us, and we must be willing, yielded vessels to bring deliverance. You might ask "How can I do this?" and my question is "How can you not do this?" We have to learn to use what is inside of us to usher the people into God's presence. But you have to know what that "it" is inside of you. Soldier, what is in your hand? Soldier, what's inside of you? Seek God, and it shall be revealed unto you. There are hidden treasures inside of you that need to be revealed.

Another way of knowing what is inside of you is knowing what is inside of your heart. As a man thinketh in his heart so is he. That tells me that we first must see ourselves as Kingdom Warriors on the inside before we can live it out on the outside. We have to know in our heart that we are Kingdom Warriors. You must have a heart of a warrior on the inside of you. The heart is the true seat of everything that warriors are. Where your heart is, is where you really are. As Kingdom Warriors we are not to be called weak, but we are called out as warriors and are more than conquerors. This is where the heart of a warrior comes into play. If your innermost man, your heart, is set on being a warrior, you will be prepared for whatever may come your way. You will live everyday saying, "Bring it on, devil!" I have a heart of a warrior, and I know what is on the inside of me. You have to speak that you are a warrior and believe it in your heart. Once you start to speak it, ask God to search you and reveal the “IT” that is inside of you.

We all have a ministry inside of us that is needed for this war, but the key is knowing what “it” is. When God reveals to you the “it”, embrace it. A lot of times when God reveals things to us for us to use we reject it, because we think it is irrelevant. If God reveals that your “it” is a smile, then smile because every time you smile and share that smile with others, you are tearing down the Kingdom of Darkness with joy. Many people probably thought David using a sling and a rock against Goliath was crazy; but that sling and rock were David’s “it”. And it defeated the Enemy. That goes to show you that Warriors, each and every one of us has an anointing on our lives, and that “it” will bring life and hope to other people. We have a gift on the inside of us, but take time to find out what is inside of you. Because if you do not know what is inside of you, you cannot prepare properly for battle. Warriors on the inside of you is love, compassion, peace, joy, strength, and creativity to name a few. You might ask, "How do I know this?" I know if you are a child of God, He dwells inside of you, and He is all of these and much more. Knowing what's inside of you is crucial during this battle. Warriors, it is time to get in your secret place and hear the voice of the Lord. Your Creator made you so He knows exactly what is inside of you, so take some time with the Creator so He can show you just what that "it" is inside of you.

Discussion/Self Check

1. Do you know what the "it" is inside of you?

____

2. If not, what are your steps to find out?

____

____

3. Are you using your "it" for this spiritual war?

____

____

____

Prayer

Lord, help me to focus and hear You clearly so I can know what You have placed inside of me to use for this War. And when You show me, Lord help me to be able to use it for what You have intended it to be used for and that is to tear down the Kingdom of Darkness. Help me to hear Your small still voice and not get distracted by what others may say. Give me the spirit of discernment to be able to detect if it is coming from You. It is so, and so it shall be, in the Mighty, Matchless Name of Jesus!

Chapter Four

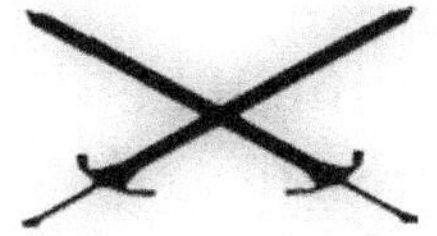

TIME TO TRAIN WARRIOR!

There is a war going on around us today, and the stakes are very high. There is war going on in the minds and hearts of people. The end results mean everything. How you minister this season in this war is the key because it can mean heaven or hell, life or death, darkness or light, freedom or slavery, and reward or punishment. Being trained as a kingdom warrior God designed you to be, means a life of commitment. It means the embrace of discipline, study and it means long intense training sometimes at the sacrifice of comfort and convenience. When you are God's warrior it means you understand the principles, and it means you will not compromise them. I am not saying it is easy, but it can be done, through proper training. Proper training will enable you to be the designed Soldier that God has designed you to be. Proper training, will teach you how to pray instead of becoming prey. Proper training will teach you how to stand bold and be the warrior you are called to be.

Kingdom Warrior, you have to realize that we have a real enemy, with real weapons and with a real plan. We cannot be ignorant of this war that is going on. The Hebrew word for ignorance is darkness. So we cannot be in the dark when it comes to us waging in war. We must be the light. The Enemy wants to gain control of your mind. If he can gain control of your mind he knows the rest of you will follow. But I ask you, why are you retreating? Why are you stepping back? Why are you stepping away? Why aren't you dancing, Warrior? Why aren't you singing, Psalmist? Why aren't you praying, Warrior? Why aren't you preaching, Preacher? Why aren't you playing the sound from heaven, Music Minister? ***Why aren't you ministering?***

This is not the time to be at ease.

"Woe to them that are at ease in Zion".

Amos 6:1

Like it or not, all of us are caught up in this spiritual war that is taking place. If you choose not to engage in this war, you are still effected by it, and if you are not training to be the Warrior God designed you to be, then you will be more vulnerable in this war. So now is not the time to be passive. Now is the time to get your training so you can be active in this war that is going on. We have to prepare before the Enemy hits us. We have to remember that just as the devil is a relentless fighter, we must also be relentless. We need to be relentless spiritual warriors waging war not against our sister or brother in Christ but against the Kingdom of Darkness. We need to be relentless spiritual warriors. Relentless spiritual warriors that have an alertness to the activity of the Enemy. But it is hard for us to be relentless spiritual warriors when we do not know how to use the spiritual tools God has given us in ministry. That is why training is very important.

In the military, a soldier is well trained and equipped in the art of waging war. Before the soldier is ready to face battle, they would have spent many long hours in basic training. They will have been prepared physically and mentally to deal with the realness of combat. The soldier will have learned how to identify the enemy and his tactics. The soldier understands that to battle against his enemy he/she will be very skilled using the tools of his/her trade. As a soldier in the military, you will be continually strengthened mentally and physically through ongoing training. The reasoning the military does this is because they want the soldier to grow constantly in job skills, new equipment training, and leadership training. In the military, they want you to constantly evolve into a smarter and more capable soldier. In God's Army, He wants you to be the same way, Warrior. He wants you to always grow in your job skills, equipment/weapons training, and leadership training. The purpose of training is to help us in this war. Training helps us understand what being a warrior is all about. God wants us to know how to lay hands and heal the sick, He wants us to know how to move in the POWER that He has given us.

Kingdom Warrior, you need proper training before you can tear down the Kingdom of Darkness. In the military, you have to qualify with a weapon and pass a physical training test before you can even graduate from basic training. They just don't hand you a weapon and expect for you to know how to use it. They train you on the weapon and the functions of the weapon. And you must go to the range and qualify with that weapon. Qualifying means you have met all the necessary requirements and have the knowledge of that weapon. As a warrior you need to qualify with your weapons. You must meet all the necessary requirements and have knowledge of the weapons. Just like it is in the natural, in the spirit we have weapons that are given to us to use, but we must be trained. We must know the functions of the weapons we use so they can be used for their intended purpose and be used to full capacity.

Before you even learn how to shoot the weapon, you need to know how to hold the weapon properly. You need to make sure your target is in view. You need to know how to aim and have a steady hand when firing your weapon. You need to know proper breathing techniques; you need to know how to aim and shoot from different positions. You need to know your environment so you can have on the proper uniform and you also must clean your weapons and check the maintenance on your weapons so that they function properly. They train for different types of scenarios that might happen. They train with different weapons, they train, train and train. Because in reality how can you survive in a war zone with no military training. How can you survive in this spiritual war zone without training? The answer to both of these questions are simple. You can't. You cannot survive without the proper training. You will die or you will be the cause to have others around you to die. We do not want to lead our sisters and brothers astray because we are not properly trained. When you are training in God's Army that means you are seeking something greater and you have told the Enemy that you have overcome your weakness and fear and moving to be the Kingdom Warrior that God has designed you to be. Warrior, this training will change you for the better. This training will transform you and this training will inspire you. This training will give you the boldness to call out Satan when you see him and cast him back to the pits of hell.

This training will also let us see ourselves and see where we are and what we need to improve on and what we need to change. This training is about looking in the mirror and seeing YOU! So when God reveals the REAL YOU, accept what is revealed and be willing to change.

But before you start basic training in the Military you must enlist. Are you ready Warrior to be trained? Have you realized that you are Soldier potential? Are you ready to enlist and join the Army of the Lord?

Discussion/Self Check

1. Why do you think training is important as you are preparing for battle?

____

____

____

____

2. Why must you remain relentless in this battle?

____

____

Prayer

Lord, as I begin this training for your Army, help me to stay focused and alert in the mighty name of Jesus! Help me to see myself clearly as You show me the REAL me. I decree that I shall not retreat, I shall not be prey of the Enemy! I shall be dedicated and focus while in training. I am ready to enlist in the Army of the Lord! I am ready to prepare for battle! I have a made up mind that I am ready to be the Warrior you have called me to be. I am ready to receive all that this training will bring to me. Amen.

Knowing Your Commander-in-Chief

The first step in tearing down the Kingdom of Darkness is knowing who your Commander is and who we are warring against. We must know our Commander in Chief. Our Commander in this spiritual warfare is Jesus. He is leading the Army of the Soldiers of the Lord. Jesus wants YOU. He wants you to choose Him and to represent Him in this spiritual war using your unique powerful dance, your unique war cry in song or your unique strategic prayer. Whatever you are gifted with, He wants you to use it for the Kingdom. He wants you to remember the power He gives you is more powerful than anything the Enemy can throw your way.

You cannot accept the call of a kingdom warrior if you have not accepted a relationship with the Father. In order to be in this Army, you have to confess with your own mouth and believe in your heart that Jesus died and rose for you that you might be saved. When you decide to serve your country through the military, you solidify your dedication with an oath. This commitment is made before a soldier begins to serve. There is no difference in God's Army. You must first say your oath; you must accept Christ. Once you have accepted Christ in your life you know who is in charge, you have to surrender everything to Him and you are ready to hear and follow your orders from the Commander-in-Chief.

God has called us into His Army to fight against the Enemy in dance, in song, in minstrels and in prayer just to name a few. Whatever God has equipped you with that is what is needed to fight against the Enemy. He leads us into battle. My question is, if you are not sold out for Christ, who are you taking orders from? You can only serve one master. If you do not have a relationship with Christ and if Christ is not your Commander-in-Chief, He is not giving you any orders. It is amazing to see so many people who want to WAR in dance, in song, in prayer, or get someone delivered that do not have a sincere relationship with the Commander-in-Chief. Before you accept any calling on tearing down any walls of darkness you first have to be rooted in a personal relationship with the Father. How can you expect a drawing when you are not connected? We as Kingdom Warriors have to be followers of Christ and follow His orders. How can you serve and follow instructions or orders when you do not know who you are serving? You must have a relationship with Him, so you can be directed and most importantly have protection. You have to have to be partnered with Christ; there is no other way to WAR. When you enlist in the Army of the Lord, you have a desire to want to know who your Commander is and you want to know His dislikes and His likes. Your job is to follow orders of your Commander. Our job as a warrior is to find out what God wants us to do and DO IT!

You have to continue to draw nigh to the Father on a daily basis and He will draw nigh to you. We are in His army and we must position ourselves to be able to hear Him so we can follow and receive orders on how to tear down the Kingdom of Darkness. Not only do we need to know how to follow instructions, we need to follow through with those instructions. Soldiers have to be doers of the Father's Word and not just hearers. We, as Kingdom Warriors, have to learn to pray, yield and obey our Commander-in-Chief. When we submit to our Commander's orders we will resist the enemy's tactics and ideas and the Enemy will flee. When we resist Satan and the evil spirits who work with him by submitting our lives completely to God, we are rejecting pride, we are refusing fear, we are praying for miracles, we are being content with Christ, we are remembering what's true and what's not, and we are never giving up when while praying. We are committed! We are becoming ready for battle!

When you truly want to know your Commander in Chief, you truly learn to surrender your will to God's will. You are committed to God and you are committed to His orders for you. Getting to know the Father is drawing nigh to Him. As you continue to draw nigh to Him, He will draw nigh to you. When you know the Commander in Chief and have a connection with Him, it is like a magnetic force that pulls you closer to Him. When you know who God is, you have an intimate relationship with Him. Knowing the Father is having a rooted relationship with Him. When you think about any relationships you have in the natural in order to get to know them, you had to spend time with them. Before my husband and I got married we spent time to get to know each other. We took time to talk and learn each other's likes and dislikes. We made time for one another to share concerns, to encourage one another, to love on one another. We grew as friends and more deeply to become husband and wife. And even after twenty-five years of marriage, we still spend time with each other because we still want to draw closer to each other. We still make time for one another, to love on one another, and to continuously learn each other. This is one of the components that helps to strengthen us and keep us connected to one another. Warriors, it works the same way with God. You have to spend time daily with Him. Get to know Him by His word. You have to observe His characteristics and His ways. As you get to know Him, you will begin to learn His ways. Knowing our Commander-in-Chief is accepting His invitation to join Him in His Army. Once we accept His invite, we make a conscious decision to follow His commands all the days of our lives. Our obedience to the Commander always brings blessings. As we continue to get to know our Commander, our knowledge of Him will deepen and our ability to trust and obey Him will begin to increase. This is the beginning of truly getting to know the Commander.

As we are in this war it is imperative that we stay connected with our Commander. Our Commander gives us direction and He protects us. We must remain connected and never depart from Him. When you are connected and know the Commander-in-Chief, you are in tune with Him. You are able to hear Him clearly.

Being able to hear Him clearly could make the difference between life and death in this war.

Warriors we should also be in tune with our Commander just in case He changes up the battle plan or gives us a new command at any given time. Once we become a part of this great Army, we have to let go of things that are trying to hinder us and our ability to hear from our Commander. We cannot let the Enemy use our past to detour us from getting a deeper relationship with our Commander. The Enemy will try to use your past to keep you from knowing your Commander or keep you from getting closer to your Commander. Know that since you have enlisted in God's Army, you are connected to Him and old things are passed away. You are a new creature WARRIOR. It is time to follow our Great Commander who is El Gibbor. The Mighty God! He is the Mighty God who fights our battles and WINS!!!

Discussion/Self Check

1. Do you have a personal relationship with the Commander in Chief? ______________________

2. How do you stay connected to the Commander in Chief? ______________________

____

____

Get Free, Be Free and Stay Free Warrior!

After we have accepted Christ, we need to let go of some things that are a hindrance. We must get free and we must stay free if we are going to tear down the Kingdom of Darkness through ministry. Whom the Son set "free "is free indeed! We have to be free.

The dictionary defines free as, not under the control or in the power of another; able to act or be done as one wishes. Without cost or payment. Since Jesus has paid the price we are free to be free. We are free, meaning when you minister you are not under the control of the world or the heaviness that may be going on around you.

Heaviness can affect us all differently, and most of us sometimes do not even know what type of heaviness is weighing us down. The spirit of heaviness is not necessarily about the weight, but about the load and how long you have been carrying the load; which in return restricts you from being able to minister freely to tear down the Kingdom of Darkness. You can only carry a five-pound weight for so long until it starts to have an effect on you. How can you minister freely if your load is hard, difficult to bear, severe or intense? The spirit of heaviness loads you down, it smothers you, and it keeps you in bondage so you are not able to see or hear clearly. You are moving, but in shackles and after a while those chains will tire you out. Can you just imagine putting chains over your entire body and trying to minister? After a while you will be tired; you will be restricted on where you can move, and how far you can move. Depending on how long the chains are, you may just injure yourself and others while ministering. When we are ministering in chains there is no way to control the chains and now the chains are in charge of ministering instead of you allowing God to be in charge. The chains because they are so long will hit everyone that is around you. Now because you have decided to minister in chains you have hurt everyone that you have come in contact with instead of you helping everyone you come in contact with. How can we minister with chains all around us warriors? How can we tear down anything being restricted in shackles? How can we move to the destination or to the person our Commander-in-Chief has ordered us if we are limited or restricted because of our own bondage. The answer is we can't. The spirit of heaviness binds us up physically and spiritually. We must put on the garment of praise for the spirit of heaviness, so we can minister freely with nothing restraining us. No worries, no flesh, no stress. Nothing is controlling you except your Commander in Chief. As Soldiers, we are called to be and move freely to help our sisters and brothers who are bound. Your Commander has orders for you. Can you hear Him, or are you too bound to hear?

When you minister, Kingdom warrior, it breaks chains! It breaks inner locks and brings us out of various prisons. It reveals to us our bondages and offers a way out of them. It shows to us what kind of bondages we have and helps us to break them! That is why we must be able to hear from the Lord so that we can break the chains off our own lives before we go before the people and minister. When God moves you to break the chains and tear down the walls of darkness through the ministry He has given you, your ministry to the prisoner says: Come out to the freedom! This ministry becomes a powerful weapon to pull down strongholds in the area of the mind, and to bring light to various areas of the soul. Being able to hear from our Commander is important because when the light comes, it brings freedom, it breaks chains and it tears down strongholds!

There is a freedom that comes when we are obedient to our Commander. *You can let go and let God.* He uses every single part of your body to express all types of emotions. We are free to worship! We are free to laugh, we are free to cry, we are free to jump and we are free to leap. We are free to have an unrestricted praise. The reality is that when you minister in total freedom you don't have to worry about a ball and chain of stress weighing you down; you don't have to worry about a ball and chain of life weighing you down. A ball and chain while ministering will take a toll on our minds and our inner being and we will forever remain in bondage if we are not careful. And I believe we as ministers have all been through something that once have had us bound. I believe that you never really understand what freedom is until you have been in bondage and realized that you were in bondage.

My family and I took a car trip that involved a lengthy drive. My granddaughter, who had just turned one, was required to sit in a car seat for the durations, fourteen and a half hours. Needless to say, she was trapped; she was not free to move around and about like she normally could. I can only imagine how she felt in the car seat. She was limited in movement. She could only lift her head, arms, and legs so far. She could only turn so far. She was not able to fully engage with everything going on in the car due to the restraint of the car seat. I understand that today there is a lot of people who do not know what freedom is. They are spiritually stuck, running in circles or even running in place wasting a lot of time yet moving nowhere. Stuck like my grandchild. When we took her out of the car seat to change her diaper, she smiled. She was happy. She was free. She had a new demeanor and understood what it meant to be free. After the taste of freedom, she did not want to get strapped down again. Warriors that is why it is important for us to get free, be free and stay free so that we might minister to others in freedom. We as Soldiers preparing for battle cannot be chained to our nature and desires. We have to be about the Father's business. Once we have accepted Christ, we have accepted truth and freedom. Being free is a benefit of being a Soldier of the Army of the Lord. That is why it is so important to know and listen to your Commander so that you might be so moved by the freedom of the ministry inside you that you cannot help yourself from the Lord taking over the ministry, orchestrating and directing everything. Be free to minister with boldness if He needs you too. If you are in shackles and not free, it's hard to express how you really feel. Something is always holding you back, something is always wrapping you up. What is that "something" that is keeping you from ministering freely warrior? When we minister we are not a slave to the Enemy. We are kingdom citizens!

Be free and minister because God enables you to reach beyond the natural, step into the supernatural and bring the same heavenly fragrance to earth through an anointed movement, song or sound. Meaning, you surrender your all to God and you are yielding to His spirit. It is not by might, nor by power but by His Spirit. We have to be free so that His Spirit can move so that His spirit can help free ourselves and others around us. Who ever knew that with each time you minister God takes you to a new level of freedom? God literally blows a fresh anointing of freedom upon your spirit and you are free to move. Have you ever felt the Lord kiss you with freedom? It's an amazing feeling. You literally feel the shackles fall off of you.

Warriors when you are able to minister in freedom it releases you from your "self" and produces a real surrender freedom deep within the soul. Being free is when you surrender your flesh and disrobe the garment of "self". When you disrobe the garment of "self" you can really let God move you freely. Garment of "self" is when you think that it is all about you and that is when the spirit of pride creeps on in. And when the spirit of pride creeps in, it will soon take over and you can't minister freely Warrior. You let go of the Fathers hand and put the garment of "self" on. Never let go of the Father's hand while ministering. Be free in God! This is critical in our training because once you let pride creep in, the Enemy will continue to boost your ego and now you become a threat to the assignment God assigned you too. Your ministry then becomes entertainment. Remember Warriors it is the anointing that destroys every yolk, not the entertainment. Be free to be "FREE".

Now the Lord is the Spirit, and where the Spirit of the Lord is, there is freedom.

2 Corinthians 3:17

Warrior, if you are not ministering in the spirit of God, you are ministering in the spirit of bondage. If you are not ministering in freedom, you are moving *out* of the spirit of God and moving *into* the spirit of bondage. Satan uses bondage to restrict us. Satan will use any and everything to weigh you down.

The Spirit of the Lord is upon me for he has anointed me to bring Good News to the poor. He has sent me to proclaim that captives will be released, that the blind will see, that the oppressed will be set free, and that the time of the Lord's favor has come

Isaiah 61:1-2; Luke 4:18-19

When you minister, you need to cling to God's word, you are free. Jesus came to set us free. So we can go out and minister freely in the privacy of our home or in a public setting. You can worship our Savior freely because He has given us the power to stand boldly and minister with power and authority. So when the world wants to label you as a failure, a doubter, a hopeless sinner, someone depressed, someone oppressed or poor, you can lift your head to the hills where your help comes from because all your help comes from the Lord and begin to leap and jump because God says, you are a Child of Promise, you are free to be "Free". We must be free to worship. When you are free you understand that God adores you, He loves you, and releases you to minister freely. He is a loving Father who delights to watch you minister, Warrior. So Warrior, arise and know that freedom is a benefit that comes when you enlist in this Army.

Knowing and ministering in freedom is totally up to you. We have to realize that we are free to minister because we have an awesome relationship with the Father. We are free to be "Free". That is the truth, and nothing but the truth. It is the truth whether you believe it or not; it is truth whether you feel it or not. That is the truth, and nothing but the truth. When we are ministering freely before the Lord we cannot rely on our feelings but on His every Word. If we relied on our feelings, we would be in bondage and would only give out in ministry what our feelings would want to give out. See, when we rely on God's Word, we stand on His Word and move under the unction of the Holy Spirit. We are free to be "FREE". Free to move, free to spin, free to jump, free to sing, free to pray and free to leap. The Word tells us that there is a time to for everything. So why aren't you singing, dancing or praying in freedom when all hell breaks loose around you? Why aren't you dancing, singing and praying your way to victory? When we are yoked up to the King of Kings and Lord of Lords, we can be set free from every bondage and shackle of the Enemy. Time to ARISE KINGDOM WARRIOR!

You are free to be "FREE", but if you are not free how can you get free? Can you be the one that is holding yourself back from ministering freely? A person does not have to be behind bars to be a prisoner. People can be prisoners of their own concepts and ideas. They can be enslaved to themselves. They can hold themselves back from completely ministering in freedom, because of themselves. Sometimes we put ourselves in a cell and throw the key deep down within us, yet we are looking for others to get us out. Or sometimes we are not free because we don't know that we are in jail. See the difference between being in physical jail and spiritual bondage is in the physical you know what to expect, there is routine day planned for you. You can see yourself locked up, but in the spiritual realm, we cannot see the shackles and chains binding us up. We do not know that we are in confinement in our minds and bodies. We don't see the Enemy holding us back but we feel the pressure of things weighing us down. But God says if you would just pray, dance or sing your way out, you will find the key. While Paul and Silas were in the physical prison, they still experienced spiritual freedom. They were surrounded with despair, but chose to wear their garment of praise. This ultimately led to their physical freedom. This is why we cannot allow any person, obstacle, or circumstance to become a weight that limits us or deters us from the path in which God has set for us. We have to learn that we can minister freely because even when it seems like the darkest hour of our life, the midnight hour, God reveals that this is not the darkest hour but it is the hour of revelation, the hour of power, the hour where you will leap into a new level of freedom. This makes me want to shout from the top my lungs, I am free to be "FREE"! Free to be FREE! The sound of freedom rings in the spirit, so we have to walk in it, Warrior. You are FREE!

Stand fast therefore in the liberty were with Christ has made us free, and be not entangled again with the yoke of bondage.

Galatians 5:1

Discussion/Self Check

1. What spirit creeps in when you put on the garment of self?

____

2. Has there ever been a time in your life when you wore the garment of "self"? If so, what actions did you take to disrobe the garment of "self"?

____

____

____

____

3. Are you totally free when you minister? If not, what is holding you back?

____

____

____

____

____

____

Prayer

Father God, I accept You into my life, I decree and declare that I am free to be free when I minister. Freedom is what was given to me when I accepted You in my heart. Show me if anything is hindering me from moving forward in complete freedom, and once You show me, I ask that You remove it and fill that void with more of You. I shall not let pride creep in because I am wearing a garment of "self". Thank you God for the spirit of FREEDOM! I am ready to train for this Army Lord. I am free to be FREE. Amen.

Are You Fit To FIGHT?

Or do you not know that your body is the temple of the Holy Spirit who is in you, whom you have from God, and you are not your own? For you were bought at a price; therefore glorify God in your body and in your spirit, which are God's.

1 Corinthians 6:19-20

Are you fit to fight, Warrior or do you get tired easily? It is important to stay in good condition spiritually, physically, mentally, and emotionally. Kingdom Warriors, in order to be optimally effective when fighting, we have to take care of our natural bodies. I never did like working out, but as I continued to grow in the ministry, I would become exhausted while ministering. God spoke to me and told me I have to be in shape when it comes to ministry. When you are in the military you have to do physical training every day. This is a part of conditioning the body. Some people may not think that it is important to stay fit naturally, but as a warrior in training, it is time to GET FIT TO FIGHT! You have to be able to endure all that the Enemy is bringing your way. You have to train, train and do more training. And you have to eat healthy. You cannot be a Kingdom Warrior that runs out of breath in five minutes of the fight. You have to train and condition yourself so when it comes to battle to bring about deliverance for someone, you do not get tired. It is important for us to MOVE warriors. Warriors we have to take care of our bodies and commit to living a healthy lifestyle. Believe it or not, our staying fit and living a healthy lifestyle is being a good witness. Taking care of our health is one way we can be a good witness to others with whom we come in contact with.

The reason we want to keep our bodies conditioned to fight is so we can be always ready. We as warriors may not know what type of fight or when we will be called to go in for someone. The more we stay fit to fight, the more energy we will have. At the same time, the more energy we have, the more we can put into the assignment God has given us. We have to stay ready! We stay ready by taking care of our natural body as well as our spiritual man. We have to walk, jog or do some type of aerobics. We have to keep our bodies in a ready state for war!

We are called to take care of our temples. Be mindful of what you are putting in your temple, Kingdom Warriors. You would not put sugar or water in your gas tank and expect your vehicle to perform well. When water is in your gas tank your vehicle will have problems with acceleration and will also stall the car's engine. That is why our cars call for fuel and not water for its performance. Our cars need fuel and the right type of fuel for it to perform properly. When we look at our bodies, we need to watch what we are putting in our temples. We need to eat things that will help our engines move to the greatest level of performance. We do not want to put things in us that will slow or stall our bodies down. So warriors as we are getting ready to battle, let's learn how to put the correct things into our temple and let's avoid putting anything into our temples that will slow us down. We need to stay conditioned so that we are always ready for battle! This is how we stay SHARP!

Strong
Healthy
Always
Ready and
Prepared

Discussion/Self Check

1. Do you think it is important to stay fit? ________

____

2. How often do you work out? ________________

____

3. Are you mindful of what you put into your Temple? ______________________________

Prayer

Father God, I thank You for helping me to understand the importance of keeping my temple conditioned and being mindful of what I put into my temple. I am committed to staying ready so when You call me I do not have to get ready! Amen.

Chapter Five

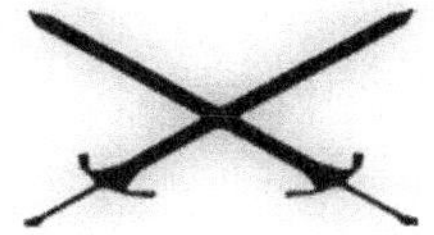

WEAPONS TRAINING

We as warriors need to know the difference between our armor and our weapons. They are not the same thing. Both are designed to do something different. Armor is designed to protect you, and you do not take it off to fight the enemy. You fight with it on. The moment you take off your armor, you leave yourself vulnerable to the Enemy. On the other hand, weapons are designed to inflict damage, injure and to wound the enemy. Your weapons are designed to make him incapable of continuing his mission. In the Military before you can use a weapon, you have to be trained on the weapon. You have to learn how to hold and position the weapon correctly. If you do not learn how to use your weapon properly, you will not use it to its full capability in order to tear down the Kingdom of Darkness or you can hurt your comrade. You can hurt your comrade by shooting your weapon in the wrong direction or just not knowing how to fire your weapon and your comrade is depending on you to use the weapon that you have in your hand.

What are your weapons in the Kingdom? Do you know the functions of your weapons? Do you know when and what weapons to use for the different type of battles you may encounter? It is very important to know what your arsenal tools are. If you do not know what they are or how they are used, then you will not use them properly and the Enemy will have you frustrated. Being trained as a Kingdom Warrior is not easy, so we must train to be efficient with our weapons. In the military they always try to get the upper hand against their enemy by creating and designing new and improved weapons. Well in the Army of the Lord, God has given us weapons to fight our enemy forces, but we have to know what they are and know how to use them. What weapons are you packing? Do you perform daily maintenance checks on your weapons?

THE WEAPON OF PRAYER!

I like to think of prayer as a secret weapon. Shooting arrows of prayer is a sure way to tear down the Kingdom of Darkness. Your prayers are powerful and have awesome range, Warrior. That is why we must train ourselves to pray. We must get grounded in the word, so we know what to pray and how to pray. We should think of our prayer closet as a foxhole. A foxhole is a hole in the ground used by troops as a shelter against enemy fire or as a firing point. So our prayer closets are foxholes because we are shooting off prayers that are backing the enemy forces up. We are covered in the safety of the Master's arms. Warrior's prayers are prayers that are intense because we know that there is a war going on and people lives are at stake. These prayers are damaging the Enemy's camp.

The bible tells us to pray without ceasing. It is important to pray without ceasing because prayer is a dynamic tool against the Enemy. When I use the term *pray without ceasing*, I do not mean you have to be on your knees praying 24 hours, seven days a week. But we should always have an attitude of prayer. The weapon of prayer is one weapon that the Enemy does not have and the Enemy **cannot** stop. When it comes to the weapon of prayer the Enemy does not have a defense for this. The effectual fervent prayers of the righteousness availeth much. We must have discipline to pray. We must be disciplined to pray when we get up in the morning. We must be disciplined to pray when everything is going well, and we must be disciplined to pray when all kind of hell is breaking out. Prayer is a vital weapon when you are in WAR.

Prayer is a way to communicate with the Lord. Just like in the military, we had a set time for training every day so that our body is conditioned. So must you, when you pray and you train to be a Kingdom Warrior. You must have a set time to train yourself to pray, so your spirit man is conditioned. Especially if you are just beginning to build your prayer life. You need to make an appointment with God; put Him on your calendar. If you do not have a set time, then you will put the training off easily for other things. Make God a priority in your life when it comes to training yourself in prayer. Setting aside time is the most important place to begin to train yourself and develop your prayer life. If you never take time out to pray, your prayer life will never grow, and you never train for the WAR. Your weapon of prayer will never develop.

You must remember as you are in this training phase, that you cannot start out with unrealistic goals. Start off with a time that you are willing to commit to. If you are not willing to commit some of your time to prayer then you have already lost this battle. We have trained ourselves to do a lot of things, but the most important thing we need to make sure we are doing is praying. We cannot survive in this war without prayer. We cannot be the warrior God designed us to be if we are not prayer warriors. It is essential for us to raise prayer to a high priority in our lives so that it becomes a daily habit. Prayer should never be mechanical, but it should be disciplined. The reason we need training in prayer is because prayer adds structure to our lives. With prayer it encourages us and sprouts seeds for us to grow in the Father.

PROPER TRAINING IN PRAYER:

- Prepares us for what is to come.
- Prepares us for any situation.
- Loads us up with ammunition for battle.
- Teaches us discipline and trains us on how to stand on the word of God. Proper training in prayer is mandatory training for this spiritual WAR.

We need to train ourselves to pray. But in order to train and discipline ourselves to pray, we have to fully understand **WHY** prayer is important. If we do not understand the **WHY** or the **importance** of a thing, then we will not take it on.

Jesus prayed not only to set an example for us, but He prayed to teach us that even the Son of God needed to be connected through prayer to God. He was teaching us that prayer was an important factor to spend time with the Father, to be effective in ministry, and to deal with the WAR. Even the Apostles knew the importance of prayer. They asked Jesus to teach them how to pray. We must remember prayer is not a formula or a code but one heart talking to another, it is expressing our sincere desire to know the heart of God. We also have to remember as we are praying, it is also a time of listening. God is giving us strategic moves and actions to take during this time. First, in prayer we must learn how to be quiet and be still. We cannot always just talk a mile a minute in our prayer time with God. We must take time to sit and listen to what the Father is telling us. He is teaching us to wait and be patient while we are waiting on the Father to speak. It is very important that we learn in prayer to be still and know that He is God.

We must understand that this training in prayer is not automatic. It is all about personal discipline. We must want this training; we must pursue this training. As Kingdom Warriors we must have a heart and passion for prayer. Prayer is a necessity in training. You cannot live without prayer. The need for prayer never ceases and as Kingdom Warriors, we should avail ourselves to prayer at all times. This is our duty. Prayer is part of your spiritual food that is needed to survive in this war. I am sure you have heard the saying, "pray or be prey". The Enemy will prey on you daily if you are not in your war room (foxhole) praying. We as Kingdom Warriors need to understand that we are at war, and our prayers should indicate that we are in war.

Prayer is a lifeline and strength of a kingdom warrior fighting to tear down the walls of darkness. Once you begin to pray, you will become more spiritually aware so you will recognize when you or your sisters or brothers in Christ are under attack. Through prayer, God will give you strategic ideas and plans on how to defend yourself against any assaults from the Enemy. Many today are trying to fight this spiritual battle with carnal, worldly weapons. You are never going to win this spiritual fight fighting this way. Jesus has given you authority to pray in His name and to know that He will answer your prayers according to God's will and at the right time. Be confident that you can pray to usher God's power into any situation. Prayers will fill you up and make sure you are not running on empty. Your spirit man cannot run on empty, Warrior. If you are on empty, you cannot move. And you are in danger of becoming a casualty in this war.

We must pray at all times to keep us filled and to seek God for guidance. We must also pray in the Holy Ghost. Praying in the spirit reminds you that you are a child of God and that you have a right to pray in the spirit to cry out to the Most High God.

For ye have not received the spirit of bondage again to fear; but ye have received the Spirit of adoption, whereby we cry, Abba, Father. The Spirit itself beareth witness with our spirit, that we are the children of God.

Romans 8:15-16

Praying in the Holy Ghost builds you up.

But ye, beloved, building yourselves on your most holy faith, praying in the Holy Ghost.

Jude 1:20

When you are praying in the Holy Ghost it builds yourself up, to let you know that because you are connected to Him, you know who you are and the power that dwells inside of you. Praying in the Holy Ghost confuses the Enemy. It produces a supernatural power. It releases things that you do not know what to pray with your own natural language. The Holy Spirit is your prayer partner. It links up with you to do powerful things and you have powerful results. Warrior your prayer linked to the Holy Spirit is vital because it enhances your prayer. It is like the super charger on your weapon of prayer. It builds up your faith. Prayer and the Holy Spirit goes hand in hand. The thing about this enhancer is that you must pray so that the Spirit can dwell inside of you. You have to be a Soldier that pray and pray in the Spirit because it takes more than just putting on your armor you must also pray in the spirt warrior. When you pray in the spirit you are releasing a direct connection to the heavens and you are calling on prayers with supernatural power to do supernatural things. When we are praying in the spirit we are no longer operating or functioning in the natural.

READY FOR BATTLE!

When we pray we are we are preparing our hearts and minds for battle. When we are praying in the spirit it gives us direction. When you use the weapon of prayer it allows you to use the word as a mass weapon of destruction. In order for you to be qualified to use this mass weapon of destruction you have to be a praying man or woman of God. If not, you will not use it properly. Our prayers should never be an afterthought meaning prayer should always be the one driving us or steering us because the Holy Spirit is leading the way. **PRAYER changes things, PRAYER pushes things, PRAYER breaks things and PRAYER up roots things.** Warriors your weapon of prayer is powerful. Let's begin to use the weapon of prayer and praying in the spirit to tear down the Kingdom of Darkness. God has given us weapons. Use your WEAPON OF PRAYER!!

Discussion/Self Check

1. How do you see prayer as an important weapon?

____

____

____

2. Why is praying in the Spirit important? ______

____

____

3. How would you rate your prayer life warrior?

____

____

____

Prayer

Father, I make a firm commitment that I will be obedient and disciplined when it comes to prayer. Help me realize that the weapon of prayer is a necessity that must be on my tool belt as a Kingdom Warrior. Help me to pray without ceasing. I pray for an increase thirst and hunger to pray your word like never ever before. I promise to keep reading, applying, obeying, loving, and sharing Your Word. Amen.

ARROWS OF DESTRUCTION/KNOWING THE WORD OF GOD

As Kingdom Warriors it is your job to know who your enemy is, to know his mission and the different tactics or methods that he may use. Your enemy is Satan, the highest ranked of the fallen angels who rebelled against God. Satan is your adversary, accuser, tempter, and deceiver. His mission is to prowl about like a roaring lion to try and to convince you to doubt God's truth and believe his lies instead. Every good Soldier will study his enemy to determine his strengths and weaknesses. And to be able to defeat the enemy, we must know how to skillfully use, with overwhelming force, the weapons at our disposal. It is time to use our arrows of destruction. Each arrow that we use is the word of God. Because we have studied our word and it is in us, our arrows are carefully crafted and molded. Our weapons are intended for flight and they are intended for Satan himself. Arrows are intended to fly and to pierce your target. As "the prince of the power of the air," he looses feelings of anger, hatred, rebellion, envy, frustration, jealousy, bitterness, resentment and competition seeking to plant these seeds into your mind. He is very sneaky, clever, cruel, relentless and experienced. He never gets tired, nor does he suffer from battle fatigue. He wants the people of God to doubt, be depressed, lose hope and be filled with un-forgiveness and resentment toward each other. He wants you to question your salvation, your calling and your assignment. These are nothing more than **"seed bombs"** being dropped and planted all around us! And if we are not in God's Word and know what arrow to shoot back, he will poke and probe for weaknesses and anything he can use against us to deceive us.

The Word of God is powerful and sharper than any two-edged sword. There is power in God's Word. God's Word does damage to the Enemy when you know how to use it effectively. That is why we as warriors in training need the word of God. We need to study the Word and pray the Word of God like never before. If we are not studying God's Word how can we back up the Enemy? How can you tear down the walls of darkness if there is no Word in you? What we as warriors need to know is God's word has power, and it is the power in God's Word that will break shackles and bring healing and deliverance. Our arrows are designed to fly a great distance as we use the Word of God on the Enemy. There is no distance in the realm of the spirit so that is why our arrows of the word of God travel far. When I tried archery for the first time, I understood the importance of how to hold the bow and how to release the arrow. I had to be positioned correctly, and I had to know where my target was to release the arrow. The further I pulled back on the bow, the further the arrow went. This made me think of the Word of God. It reminded me of how important it is to know the Word of God and how we need to get deep in the Word. So you know what word to release over your situation. When we do not know the Word, we don't know what arrows to release. If we do not know what arrows to release, we become prey.

In the military you have to study and learn the Code of Conduct. One of the Codes of conduct talks about if you become a prisoner of war (POW) you know what information you can release and it also says you NEVER surrender. Well, in the Army of the Lord, we are given the WORD of the LORD and we are to remember it, and we are to release the arrows over our situation. We are not to surrender to the Enemy! It does not matter what situation you come across, there should be an arrow on your tool belt ready to release over the Enemy. Knowing the Word of God is sort of like what the military would call "AIR SUPPORT" when the Enemy is attacking on the ground, the troops call in Air Support to come in and take the Enemy out. That is why Warrior you need to know the Word of God so you can call in the King of Battle of Air Support!! When we feel like we are backed up by the enemy call on God, and He will launch arrows of fire to put the Enemy to flight. Train Warrior! Train Warrior! Study the Word of God Warrior! Your destiny depends on it!

There is a war going on and it is time to arise and release those fiery arrows to tear down the Kingdom of Darkness. Release the arrows of destruction over your life, release it over your family's life, and release it over your ministry. It is time to release arrows, Soldier. It is time to release the arrows of destruction over every seed bomb the Enemy has planted over your ministry. You shall live and not die. When you release the arrows of the Word, you are doing critical damage to the Enemy.

When you release the Word of God out of your mouth, they become arrows of destruction. This is the time God is calling every Kingdom Warrior to grab their bows and arrows, and God is saying "RELEASE IT!" Our words are arrows, and our tongue is the bow that is used to release these arrows. The Word of God that we release can bring critical injury to the Enemy we are fighting against. Study the Word of God Warrior so that it is in you to pull out and use during this war.

Discussion/Self Check

1. What are "seed bombs"? ____________________

____

2. What will destroy the "seed bombs? __________

____

3. Are you comfortable with releasing arrows of destruction for every situation?_________________

____

____

____

FASTING

Fasting is an awesome spiritual weapon because it is a way to connect to God like no other. Fasting is a way we kill our selfish desires and offer a sacrifice to our Savior. Sometimes when we are in battle, we can get overwhelmed, and our flesh will want to rise up. Because of this, we can make all kinds of hasty decisions; but with prayer and fasting, we can get in a place where we can kill the flesh, and our spirit will become more sensitive to the Father for direction and guidance. As Warriors we must never let the voice of our flesh out power the voice of God. Fasting on a regular basis keeps us focused.

When I was in the military, I remember when I went to the range I had to zero my weapon. When you zero your weapon, you are aligning your weapon to your individual site so you can be able to hit the target. As we look at fasting, we can say that fasting is a way of zeroing ourselves so that we can get back in alignment with God and so He can give us what we need to hit our target. We need to make sure we are zeroing ourselves so we can get refreshed, revived and restored in this battle.

When we look at fasting we need to see it as a way that the spirit is able to speak to us without distractions. In this war zone we need to be in a place where we can hear God's voice and detect when He is moving because our very lives depend on it. We want to always go with God! Fasting is a weapon we all need to use frequently because we need to make sure we are sensitive to the Holy

Spirit in this war. Sometimes in the war you must use fasting *and* prayer. The bible speaks of the disciples could not cast the demon out, but when Jesus came down from the mountain He told the disciples that "this kind can come out only by prayer and fasting". Fasting was a part of Jesus' life and since we are created in the Father's image and display His characteristics, fasting should be a part of our lives, Warriors.

Fasting is not dieting. Fasting is a sacrifice. Warriors, fasting will increase your hunger for God, and as a warrior, our appetite should always be hungry for God. As we are fasting and realigning ourselves, things inside of us are awakening. God is speaking and revealing things to us about this war. He is redeveloping us. Fasting also lets us know that we cannot get by without the Father. It draws us close to the Father and in return He draws closer to us. As warriors in training, fasting is a weapon that trains us in self-control. Warriors have to have self-control during the war and have a clear mind and vision to function properly. This weapon builds up our faith muscles so that we can withstand the things the Enemy throws our way.

With fasting you have to start small if you never fasted before. You have to build yourself up first, you must train yourself and remember to always consult with your physician if you are on any type of medication or you are under health care. Also there are different type of fasts and you will need to make sure that you choose which one is right for you. As warriors we will need to take time to abstain from certain foods and activities and spend that time in the Word of God. God is looking for warriors who are serious about training up to tear down the Kingdom of Darkness. Are you truly committed to fasting? Are you that warrior that He will call on because He sees that you are fasting for a deeper relationship with Him? Are you that warrior that He will call on because you are seeking His heart and not just His hand?

PRAISE IS A WEAPON

Praise is a necessity for every Warrior. God inhabits the praises of His people. When we as warriors praise God we invite God's mighty deliverance power to move upon us and those who are around us. This weapon of praise is the access to the presence of the Most High God.

When you praise God you are telling Him your exact coordinates, and He comes on the scene and binds the Enemy. Warriors, we have to begin to praise in such a manner that it causes the Enemy to turn around and run back to the pits of hell from which he came. Warriors never lose their PRAISE! Praise is your weapon. The Enemy wants you to drop your weapon of praise down and never use it again. He knows if we lose our weapon of praise, we will lose our joy. Warriors never let your praise die! When we use our weapon of praise we are actually taking our eyes off the battle, and we are seeing the victory! We are letting God know that we have faith in Him, and we know we have the VICTORY! When we use our weapon of praise, we are lifting our eyes to the hill from which cometh all our help. Warriors, we should love to release a sound of praise in the atmosphere because it confuses the Enemy. When you open up your mouth and release a loud and vigorous praise, it strikes fear in the Enemy.

There are many ways to use praise as a weapon. Think on what you can use to release a praise and then release it. Praise involves your hands, your mouth, playing an instrument and dancing. Your whole body can be used as a praise weapon.

HANDS - Warriors you can clap, raise your hands, and wave your hands. When you use your hands as a weapon of praise, it is literally shaking up things in the spirit. It is realigning things and putting them back into their proper places. When we use our hands to clap we are making sounds of thunder! We are releasing a sound of thunder to break down every barrier that the Enemy is building. Putting your hands together is creating a sound in heaven that will destroy the plots and plans of your Enemy. Warriors putting your hands together creates a disturbance in the Enemy's camp. Let's Go Warriors! Let's begin using our hands as weapons of praise. We are getting ready for battle; we are getting ready to tear down the Kingdom of Darkness with our hands.

MOUTH - With your mouth you can open up and release a sound from heaven that makes the Enemy flee from your camp. Warrior when you open up your mouth with a loud praise it will release a sound of victory that will silence the very mouth of the Enemy. Remember the Jericho walls fell only after the Israelites marched around the city, blew the trumpets and shouted! When you shout, Warrior, the very walls that the Enemy has built will be crumbled to pieces. Walls are coming down when we open our mouths and use it as our weapon. Let's open our mouths and give the Lord a SHABACH. Warriors we have to be comfortable with shouting. When up against the Enemy, if you begin to let a shout out of your mouth you will continuously confuse the defeated foe. Remember that YOUR PRAISE is YOUR WEAPON. We must use our own mouth to praise God. We cannot depend on the singer or our neighbor, we as kingdom warriors have to open up our own mouths and sing our praises to the Lord. The Enemy wants to destroy you, Warrior, so why not open up your mouth and give a praise. If you are not use to opening up your mouth and shouting before the Lord; now is a good time to get your training in. Don't' let the Enemy use fear tactics on you to keep your mouth shut. Just open up your mouth now and give God a loud vigorous shout of VICTORY. It is going to be handy when you are looking for your weapon of praise to use against the Enemy. Your own praise will confound the Enemy.

PLAYING AN INSTRUMENT - Warrior just because you might not know how to play an instrument doesn't mean you can't play an instrument for praise. You my dear warrior are the instrument. Yes, you are the instrument. You are an organ, you are a trumpet, you are a guitar and you are a drum. You have vocal strings, and you have feet. Warrior it is time to use your feet as a weapon of praise. Use your feet to stomp on the Devil's head. Use your body to make a joyful noise before the

Lord. Use your body as in instrument. Your body can be an orchestra to play a symphony. Warriors it is time to use your body as a weapon of praise.

DANCE - When you dance before the Lord, Warrior, the Enemy is trembling. Dance Warrior, dance. Use dance as your weapon of praise. You do not have to be a trained dancer to be able to dance before the Lord. Just imagine you are dancing with the Father and just move. God will be pleased with your dance and make things happen on your behalf. So Warrior it is time to get up and dance! Let everything that has breathe, praise ye the Lord! Warriors when you dance you are releasing a praise. I once heard someone say that praise clears the path. Meaning sometimes on this battlefield, things will get a little foggy, the winds may blow, and your vision may get a little foggy; but when we begin to dance a dance of praise, it helps us to get back on track. It helps us breakthrough and break-forth! Use your body to release a dance of praise that will cause confusion to the Enemy.

CONCLUSION

One of the praise weapons I like to use is the Mat-teh sticks to release a sound that causes disturbance and confusion to the Enemy. This word means rod. As you are releasing a sound with the Mat-teh sticks, you are actually breaking and binding things up in the spirit realm. You are showing the Enemy that God has given you the authority to release this sound. If properly trained and used correctly you can release a praise of victory over your city, over your home, over the ministry inside of you, and over your region.

As you are releasing your praise, the spirit realm is opening up and God is shifting that very weapon the Enemy was trying to form for you. God is looking for a few good warriors to release a sound of praise. Praise when used correctly is a very powerful weapon. When we praise the Lord, He is going before us and making all our enemies turn back and stumble. That is why it is important to train with our weapons of praise. Use the weapons of praise daily that God gave you. You should never look at someone else's weapons of praise and think that you can use them the same way and get the same results. You have to become qualified with YOUR weapons of praise and use YOUR weapons of praise the way God designed you. And once you become skillfully trained on the weapons God has equipped you with you are ready for battle. Let your praise with the Father become WARSHIP.

PRAYER

Father God teach me how to train with each weapon properly so that I may become skillfully trained on each weapon. Give me the wisdom to use each weapon effectually and efficiently. Father, I invite your presence into my life and as you give me greater strategic ways to help me become skilled on these spiritual weapons I stand to learn. Lord as a warrior I stand ready to battle. Amen.

CHECKPOINT

Now that you have had your weapons training, you are ready to put on the armor of God and get into position!

Put on the whole armour of God, that ye may be able to stand against the wiles of the devil. For we wrestle not against flesh and blood, but against principalities, against powers, against the rulers of the darkness of this world, against spiritual wickedness in high places. Wherefore take unto you the whole armour of God, that ye may be able to withstand in the evil day, and having done all, to stand. Stand therefore, having your loins girt about with truth, and having on the breastplate of righteousness; And your feet shod with the preparation of the gospel of peace; Above all, taking the shield of faith, wherewith ye shall be able to quench all the fiery darts of the wicked. 17 And take the helmet of salvation, and the sword of the Spirit, which is the word of God: Praying always with all prayer and supplication in the Spirit, and watching thereunto with all perseverance and supplication for all saints;

Ephesians 6:11-18

READY FOR BATTLE!

Chapter Six

PUT ON YOUR PROTECTIVE ARMOR EACH MORNING!

The bible tells us we must put on the armor of God to be able to defend ourselves against the schemes of the Enemy. God's armor is to be put on each morning we wake up. Putting on our spiritual armor every morning is a reminder that we are engaged in spiritual warfare, and we need to be protected at all times. When you put on the God's whole armor, the Enemy cannot see you. You are protected. It is God's armor that he sees, and he is frightened. That is why it is important to put on the whole armor of God every day. If we just wake up and go, we are putting ourselves in danger. It is time to suit up, Warrior!

Gird Your Loins with Truth- The ancient Soldier's belt was an essential piece of equipment. The belt was used to hold the other pieces of the armor together. The belt also allowed the Soldier to tuck his long tunic in the belt so that he was able to run and fight without worrying about the tunic. The belt was an essential part of the armor; it held everything together. Without this belt, the tunic would get in the way, and the Soldier would not have a place to hold his weapons. So when we think about girding our loins with truth we need to understand that the TRUTH is what holds us together. We have to be grounded in the truth; if we are not grounded in truth then it will be easy for us to believe whatever the Enemy is saying. Warriors must always abide in truth, this means, walking in truth, speaking in truth, and living in truth.

The truth is the word of God. God's word is truth, and the truth is the foundation of all your other pieces of armor. Gird your waist with truth by reading your Bible often, so that its truth sink deeply into your soul. Keeping those truths in mind whenever you make decisions will help guard you from deception. Satan is the father of lies, and he attacks you with lies. This piece of armor is important because truth helps you decipher lies. Warrior, if you are caught without wearing your full armor, you are left defenseless to fight against Satan's lies. Without the truths of God's promises for your life, Satan will attempt to infiltrate your mind with doubt. Satan wants to catch you without the full armor of God, so he can manipulate you. So we must not let him catch us without our armor of God on during this training phase.

If we get off track and picked apart during the training phase, we will never become ready for battle! We will always be a warrior in training. God wants us to pass the training phase. He needs us on the battle field. Warriors let's continue to wear the truth of the word of God. It prepares us for battle!

Breastplate of Righteousness- A Roman Soldier will never go into war without wearing a breastplate; so he would fasten the breastplate around his chest like a vest to protect his vital organs. If the Soldier failed to do this, then an arrow could easily pierce his heart or organ. Warriors, we have organs that need to be protected in this war. We need to protect our hearts.

God wants us to have pure hearts, loving hearts, contrite hearts, and hungry hearts for Him. For out of our hearts are the issues of life. The condition of our heart matters in this war. Our Father wants our whole heart and nothing less than that. If our hearts are stubborn, hard, or proud, we will be unable to hear Him properly. We must be warriors who live what we profess. When we put on our breastplate of righteousness we are guarding our hearts. It is God's righteousness that is protecting our hearts.

Put on the breastplate of righteousness by relying on the Holy Spirit's guidance to choose what's right; your right attitudes and actions will act like a bulletproof vest, protecting you against Satan's attacks. We do not want to take a chance of Satan piercing our hearts with pride or doubt. It is hard to war with a prideful heart. You cannot war effectively with pride in your heart. When you are warring with pride in your heart you are no longer warring for Jesus; you are against your battle buddies. We must never harden hearts towards our fellow warriors in battle. We have to always have a heart of forgiveness. We as warriors need to stick together and help each other out, not tear each other down. We are training to tear down the Kingdom of Darkness, not each other. So let's keep our hearts covered daily. God is not telling us to do anything that He has not done. He too put on the breastplate of righteousness when He went out to fight evil and corruption. That is why we are in training to get our hearts ready for battle. Our hearts have to be loving and forgiving hearts so we are free to do what God has called us to do.

Warriors, we serve a loving God because He shares His righteousness with us. And we will never know about his righteousness if we do not have the belt of truth firmly in place. If we do not have on the belt of truth then we will not understand Gods word and His righteousness and we are in danger of our breastplate malfunctioning. We do not need our breastplate to malfunction while we are on the battlefield. By wearing the breastplate of righteousness, it helps us to practice what we preach. It helps us to create a lifestyle of what we believe (the truth) in our hearts, and it will be displayed on a daily basis. So Warriors it is time to suite up with our breast plate of righteousness.

Shoe Your Feet with the preparation of the Gospel- No Soldier can properly fight a war without the correct shoes on our feet. Warriors we should never be found shoeless in this war. Shoes allow us to step and run freely without worrying about things causing injury to our feet. As warriors we should never worry about where we are stepping. If we are shoeless, this will cause distractions for us. This would cause us to tiptoe instead of walking or running with confidence. We should be walking in confidence not fear. Our feet should have on shoes that help us stand firm during this war. Soldiers, when we have peace with God, this becomes our firm foundation that makes us able to stand on firm ground. Just as shoes allow us to walk and run on rough terrain without fear, so will having the peace of God. Warriors, we have to first have the peace of God in our own lives before we can go out and spread peace to others. We must first buy into the peace before we can deliver peace.

Warriors we have to shoe our feet with the preparation of the Gospel of peace by accepting the peace that only Jesus can give you and by using that peace as an unshakeable foundation of confidence to defend yourself against evil. When we are wearing our spiritual shoes, it allows us to battle life pains, trials, and tribulations of life without fear. When we have our shoes on, we are ready to move out to spread the good news.

How beautiful are the feet of them that preach the gospel of peace and bring glad tidings of good things!

Romans 10:15

Warriors how beautiful are your feet? Are you treading peace everywhere you go? Are you spreading the good news? Or have you taken off your shoes, fighting barefoot?

In the Army of the Lord we have to keep on our spiritual shoes at all times. We never know when our Commander-in-Chief will call us on an assignment. When I was deployed to Saudi, I remember many of times I slept with my boots on just in case I had to get up and move out. Warriors are you resting and getting refreshed with your boots on or off? Warriors should never take off their boots and get comfortable. Once the boots are taken off and we get comfortable, the Enemy comes in and throws all kinds of things in our pathway to injure us. We have to always remember our spiritual boots are the God of peace Himself, and while wearing the boots of the God of peace, we are able to bruise the head of Satan. Warriors continue to shod your feet with the preparation of the gospel of peace. We are ready for battle; we are ready to lace up our spiritual boots and spread the good news to the nations. God has just sized you up for your boots, Warriors. Put them on with confidence and GO YE INTO THE WORLD, AND PREACH THE GOSPEL TO EVERY CREATURE!

Helmet of Salvation- The Roman helmet protected the Soldier's head from the attacks of the enemy. In today's army you also wear a helmet to save your head from damage. The helmet's purpose is to absorb any blows to the head. We need to always protect our head while in battle. We can survive a broken leg or arm, but a blow to the head could cause major damage. It can immobilize you. Our minds are where we wage in war. Our mind is a battlefield; it is where the Enemy attacks us, so it is imperative to wear our protective gear. When we put on the helmet of salvation, it guards our mind.

PUT ON YOUR PROTECTIVE ARMOR EACH MORNING

Satan likes to battle us in the mind. The Enemy can drop **seed bombs** of lies, doubt, and manipulation. When we are in war, we do not need to worry about mind games. There is no possible way for a warrior to be effective if their mind is lost. That is why it is very important to protect your mind. We are on a mission and we cannot afford to get sidetracked. His trick is to keep the warriors focused on "*this world*" and get us pre-occupied to let our guard down. The word tells us not to be ignorant of Satan's devices, so that is why we must wear the helmet of salvation. We need the helmet of salvation to save our minds and to keep our minds protected from the mind games of the enemy. This helmet helps us to remember that you are saved from Satan's deception and destruction and you are believing everything that the Lord says about you. We need to wear our helmet daily because it protects us from the Enemy attacks to disobey God. Warrior, the Enemy does not want you to be ready for battle, so he will mess with your mind to discourage you and get you off track. He wants to show you the fun things of this world to sway you from your training. But I decree and declare that every warrior reading this book shall continue to wear their helmet of salvation and stay on the course in Jesus Name! Warriors you must keep your helmet securely fastened and stay encouraged. You have the VICTORY! Stay focused!

Shield of Faith- The Roman Army shield was a slightly curved shield. It protected the Soldiers from spears, javelins swords, daggers, and arrows. It was also used to stun or knock the wind out of its opponent. A shield was both a defensive tool and an offensive weapon. We need our shields, Warriors. The shield is something we need to have in our hand at all times. As soon as we rise in the morning, the Enemy has planned his attack on us. God's shield of faith will guard and protect us. Faith will protect our spiritual lives. The shield of faith will protect us from every fiery dart of the enemy. This shield will absorb the attack of Satan. Warriors we have to have faith in God's power, and when we are holding the shield of faith, it will be impossible for Satan to break through the shield to attack us. As warriors we cannot fight in this war without the shield of faith. With all kinds of hell breaking out around us, we shall continue to go forward with God's shield of faith, knowing that the battle is already won. We shall hold our shield of faith with confidence because we know that our God is omnipotent.

On the middle of the Roman Soldier's shield, there was a knob called the *boss*. This was used to shove their opponent backwards. Warriors, when we use the shield of faith we can shove the Enemy backwards using the boss, using the faith that we have in God. Faith without works is dead. We have to use the faith to push the Enemy backwards, push the Enemy back with our strong faith. Our faith must produce action if we want to see results. Without our shield of faith, we are left vulnerable to the attacks of the Enemy. Warriors it is time for us to arise and join our shields together, strengthen each other and build each other up. When we join our shields of authentic faith together, we become an unstoppable Army. An Army of kingdom warriors ready for battle! Ready to tear down the Kingdom of Darkness.

Sword of the Spirit-. The sword of the spirit is the word of God. This powerful sword of the living word is able to cut through every defense the Enemy tries to raise. This powerful sword cuts down to the marrow of the bone. Warriors when we are using the sword of the spirit, nothing can withstand its ability to cut to the root of a thing and uncover the truth. As warriors it is our job to use this sword to discern the truth and follow the truth. This sword can surgically remove anything within us that is unlike God. But in order to use the sword properly, we need training. The training we need is reading the word of God and meditating on it day and night. We need to know how to handle the word (sword) properly. Once we know how to use it properly, then it will be effective in tearing down the walls of darkness. Warriors, the more we know and understand the word of God, the more effective we will be in doing His will and standing against the enemy.

Prayer

Lord, please help me to remember to put on the whole armor of God every day. Help me to study each piece and know that I need each one to successfully stand against the wiles of the enemy. Lord, teach me how to use your glorious sword effectively. Amen.

Chapter Seven

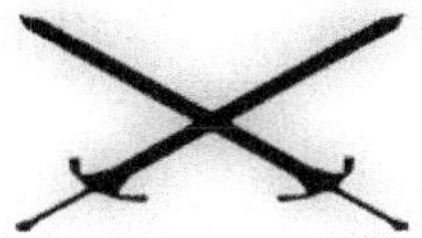

ARE YOU IN THE RIGHT POSITION?

Arise Warriors and man your position on the battlefield that God has assigned you too. Everyone is not trained to be a front line Soldier. That is why it is important to know what your rank is in this war. Some of my fellow Soldiers are going through some rough patches because they are not positioned where the Commander has placed them. They are engaging in wars where God did not place them, and in return, there are more casualties than necessary.

In the military you have officer ranks, and you have enlisted ranks. A private cannot take the position of a General when it comes to war. The private is not properly trained, and that was not his position when he enlisted. The private is not given the same authority as a General Officer, so Soldiers must stay in their proper ranks when it comes to taking orders. We have to WAIT for our assignment and train in war on the level that we are on because our very own lives depends on it. We never want to be on the Enemy's playing field because we are operating in the wrong position. It is time out for us trying to promote ourselves and mimicking what we see others do. When we mimic what others do without being told by God to do that, we are setting ourselves up for failure. We have to learn to stay in our position and wait for God to call us out and promote us.

In the military when it comes to rank and certain positions, you must train and be developed; it does not happen overnight. The same rule applies in God's Army; we must train and be developed. God equips us with what we need for the position HE places us in. We have to realize that we all are in this WAR, but we must stay and WAR in the right position. That is the only way to tear down the Kingdom of Darkness; we must all be in the correct position doing the job that God assigned us to do. There is always a value of us being in the right position, and that value is VICTORY!

When we are in the right position, we are able to function properly. Satan is busy trying to elevate you to positions that will not last. When you move out of position and get placed incorrectly, it can cripple your faith. It can cripple the Army. You will get tired and frustrated very easily, and you will not feel strong enough to even exercise your authority that you have in Christ. We as warriors must understand what authority we have and the positon we have authority in. Warriors, you will never overtake the Enemy operating in the wrong position. Trails, tribulations, and even distractions will come to get you out of positon. But stay grounded, stay determined that you will not be moved. Let the Enemy know that only God can remove you from your assigned position. You will not be moved out of nor into another position unless the Father moves you.

ARE YOU IN THE RIGHT POSITION?

When we operate in the wrong position, we get in an area where we do not have the expertise nor training to do the assigned task. If our Commander did not put us there, my question is, *who did*? Everyone in this Army has a position to which God has assigned them, and if you are not in your position, there is a hole where you should be. So if you are not where you are supposed to be, you leave a space for the Enemy to come into the camp and cause havoc. And if you stay out of position long enough, you will become to have an identity crisis. You will come to lose sight of who YOU ARE and what YOU WERE called to do. The Enemy wants you out of position, Warrior, so you will lose sight of the fact that you are a Kingdom Warrior, designed to tear down the Kingdom of Darkness in the position to which God has called you. Warrior you cannot be ignorant of Satan's devices. Stay in position and fight because you are needed. Every warrior has to realize that his position is needed, whether considered a private or a general in this Army. Warriors, you cannot listen to the enemy and let him tell you what you do is not enough, leaving you to think that you are not valuable. Every Warrior is valuable is the sight of God, and He needs YOU in this Army to be in the right position. When you are in the right position, you have the opportunity to impact lives and situations in ways that you may have never even imagined. So stay in position; you are helping building the Kingdom of God. Use the abilities that God gave you. Warrior, just because you are in position, souls will be saved and lives will be forever changed. Warrior stay in position. No one can beat you at you being you. That is why when you are in the right position, you do not have to worry about competition. You just have a passion to do what you are called to do in the position you are called to do it. That is the making of a TRUE WARRIOR, doing what they are called to in the place they are called to WAR! They understand the battlefield because they are in the right position. When you are in the wrong position the Enemy will take you to an unknown battlefield and because you have not trained or studied on this terrain, you are lost.

When you are in the wrong positon, and you are attacked by the Enemy, you are in a dangerous place, because you may not have any idea of what prayers it will take to let your buddies know what battlefield the Enemy has you on. Stay in positon! Know your battlefield! When I was in the Army, we had to become familiar with our battlefield. We had to know our surroundings and get the Enemy where we wanted him so we can defend our posts. When you are training to be the warrior God has God you to be, you have to know your battlefield. When you are in the right position you can close your eyes and know what battlefield you are on because that is your manned position. That is why you train warrior so that you know your terrain. When you are trying to operate in a position where you are not designed to operate you get pulled into the Enemy's territory. Warrior, get into the position to which God has assigned you. You are needed. We do not want you MIA (missing in action). God is wondering why you left your position.

Warriors, sometimes you have to listen to God to see if He is saying, "Right now your position is to sit and be still until I give you more instructions". During that positon of sitting still we have to be in a position of surrender, meaning we have to lay before Him in our secret place. We have to position ourselves, lying face down in prayer, or kneeling before the Father. When we positions ourselves with the Father it gives our expression of our heart. Sometimes we are out of sync with the Father, because we have not positioned ourselves before Him in a posture of prayer or worship. We need to learn the position of being still before the Father. This shows Him our heart. In this time with the Father He will show us when it is time to move out and conquer! No matter what positon He has placed you in, you must remain in that positon. Warriors are you in the right position? Even if you have wondered off, you can always find your way back to Christ, and He will put you where you belong. Thank God that we are Warriors who shall remain in position! Thank God we are Warriors who know the positon of laying before the Father.

General Orders to remind you to stay in Position

When I was in the military, we had to learn our General Orders, and I believe these general orders are a good training tool for warriors to always remember and practice to keep us where we need to be.

1. You will guard everything within the limits of your post, and you will only quit your post when properly relieved. When you are in position, you are saying, “God, I will remain here and protect everything you have assigned me to in this position, and I will only leave this positon when you tell me Lord." You are committed to guarding everything that is within the limits of your authority. Whatever position God has placed in you, you have determined that nothing shall get past you. You shall remain on alert and observe what is going in your area. No matter how you may be feeling you will not leave you post, no matter how you may be tempted or swayed by the Enemy. You will not leave until you are properly relieved by who God sends.

2. You will obey your special orders and perform all of your duties in a military manner. Warriors, God will give you what you need to complete this task while in this position. You will complete every task with the spiritual tools He has given you while in this position. You shall stay in position and do everything in excellence to your Father. You will not *half do* anything, but it shall all be done in a manner that will make God proud. Whatever orders God gives you, no matter how small or how large, it will be done in such a manner of excellence that people know that you are a Warrior who was sent by God.

3. You will report violations of your special orders, emergencies, and anything not covered in your instructions to the Commander of the Relief. Lord when things happen that I might not understand, I will not get lured by the Enemy to step into positions that I have not been trained for, I will hold my position and call on You, the Great I Am, to call in the support that I need.

Discussion/Self Check

1. Have you ever gotten out of the position God placed you in?________________________________

____

If so, how did you get back into your position?______________________________________

____

____

2. Why is it important to stay in the "right" position?

____

____

____

____

____

Prayer

Lord, please help me to understand the importance of me staying in position. As a Warrior I have committed to staying where You have placed me until I am properly relieved. I will do the assigned tasks with excellence unto You God. Lord, thank You that You see me as your child, and You say that I am valuable in what I do for the kingdom. I shall not get blindsided by the Enemy. I shall remain focused, and I shall stay in position! Amen.

CHAPTER EIGHT

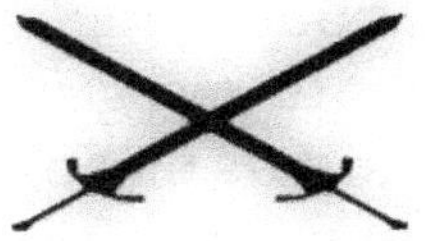

YOU WILL KEEP RUNNING AND WILL NOT FALL OUT OF THE RACE!

Warriors, sometimes we hear God telling us that He has chosen us for such a time as this, but because we are uncertain, we run away. Believe me when I tell you, you will come to a point where you get in a spiritual blockage, and you just want to stay complacent. However, I want you to know today that when you hit the stumbling block in your life, Satan is still lurking. Remember, Satan is trying to lure people into his trap in order to build an empire. He lures you into his trap when you become still, on your own island. You look all around you, and you believe that you just don't have what it takes. For many reasons good warriors fall out of the race. Sometimes the trials of life take you out of the race, for some fear pulls them out, for others' competition pulls them out of their race. Listen, Warriors, I had to go through many things in life, and I almost fell out of the race as well. May of 2014 I almost fell out of the race; it was supposed to be a glorious time for my family and me. I was graduating receiving my Doctoral Degree, and my daughter was graduating from High School. My oldest daughter and my grandchildren came to be a part of this glorious time......BUT LIFE HAPPENED! My two month old grandson passed away in our home while he was sleeping, a couple of days before our graduation. Our family went from celebrating our graduations to mourning the passing of our little Leonard Battle III. I wanted to fall out of the race. I did not want to heed the call any longer. Yet God was still calling me to minister in dance and preach the word of God. God was still sending people to me asking for prayer. I got to a point that I was fed up and really wanted to just go somewhere and sit down and say, "I GIVE UP!" I no longer wanted to heed the call of the warrior that God was calling me to. I almost threw in the towel. But nobody but GOD! He PUSHED and PUSHED until I got up and said, "I will HEED THE CALL. I WILL NOT QUIT! I WILL STAY IN THE RACE! I will GO FORTH as the Warrior you have called me to be." This very tragic ordeal for my family help mold me into the Warrior GOD DESIGNED ME TO BE! I am writing this book today because of what we went through as a family. I write this book because of the tools in this book actually kept me from falling out of the race. What the Enemy thought would destroy me, actually made me stronger! So today, I speak to your life and your current situations that may have you running from becoming the warrior God designed you to be. I say get up NOW in the mighty Name of Jesus! I say PRESS through. This is only a test you are going through. You were built for this! God will never allow more on you than you can bear. Use whatever is hindering you from moving forward to catapult you into a MIGHTY WARRIOR for God!

YOU WILL KEEP RUNNING AND WILL NOT FALL OUT OF THE RACE!

Let God shine His Guiding light on you. Don't let your current life situations, fear, and competition cause you to put your light out. It is not God's desire for any of His chosen, His children or His warriors to live in fear or to be trapped in darkness. It is time you get off your island. You will not have a lone ranger spirit. You will move forward! You have to recognize that this is a trick of the Enemy. As believers, we have to make sure that we are not ignorant of Satan devices. Not heeding the call because of trials and tribulations are a trick of the Enemy. Please know that all things work together for your good! Give it all over to God and watch Him work it out. All you have to do is just don't throw in the towel and make a sound decision to keep pressing, even when you don't understand. Keep pressing, even when you feel like your whole world has been shaken; keep pressing even when LIFE HAPPENS! Warrior, you are READY FOR BATTLE! What you thought was a setback was really a setup. Walk in your victory. Keep your head up High and never run away from the Warrior you were designed to be!

PRAYER

Father God, I thank you for a finisher's spirit. No matter what trials and tribulations that I come across, I will not fall out of this race. I will keep running. Running towards You. I will keep my eyes upon the hills, knowing that all my help comes from You. I will continue to seek You First. I will not throw in the towel. Thank You God for PUSHING me forward. I will always go with the PUSH. I am and shall always be the Warrior You designed me to be. Amen.

Chapter Nine

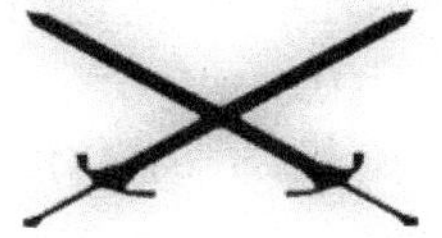

READY FOR BATTLE!

We are ready for battle to tear down the Kingdom of Darkness. We have spent time preparing for battle. So now it is time to put forth what we have been doing in our secret place. Now we are ready to move out. There are battles that you are needed for. This is not the time to be fearful because God has not given you the spirit of fear, but of love, power and a sound mind. You were called for such a time as this. The Enemy will try to tell you that you are not ready for battle, but since you are equipped and suited up with God's armor, you can shut your ear gates to the Enemy and only follow the voice of the Lord. You need to know that the Enemy will not back down. He will continue to try to get you off target. He wants you to have division with your fellow warriors, but since you have learned in training not to be ignorant of his devices, you will not fall prey to the isms and schisms that he will try to lay out before you. Warrior you are ready for battle. It is time to execute; it is time to PUSH forward. You are well able and no matter what it looks like, you have the victory. You are an overcomer; you have been given power to tread over the enemy. Stand up tall and take a good look in the mirror, you are Ready For Battle! You are a Kingdom Warrior, ready to tear down the Kingdom of Darkness.

I must warn you, Warrior, since you have completed the training and are ready for battle, there will be people and things from your past that will try to attach their selves to you to try to distract you from your mission. You must remain focused at all times because lives depend on it. You shall not be ignorant of Satan devices but allow your discernment to always be on point.

Your five senses are important warrior. Keep your eye gates closed to the things of the world and open them up to see the things of the kingdom. You see, God is always working in every battle. Keep your ear gates closed to the things of the world, but keep them open so that you may hear the frequency of the spirit. Keep your mouth gate closed to the world and open up to speak the word of the Lord. Warriors, taste and see that the Lord is good. Keep your nose gates open up to smell the sweet fragrance of the Lord. Let the sweet aroma of the Lord lead you in every battle. And Warriors, you should always let your hands touch things that are of the Lord. Do not let unholy things come near your dwelling without cleansing yourself after the touch. Only let the residue of the Holy Spirit stay upon you. Warriors, we are Soldiers, and Soldiers were made for war. We were designed to be able to carry weapons and fight. Soldier since you have taken time to train and prepare, it shows that you are committed and that you are ready for battle. The time to rise up is now Warrior. The time to answer the call is NOW! It is time to move forward in victory. Warrior, you are not defeated so you should never retreat. You serve a mighty God. Our God is greater than any other god. Warriors you have the power of the Holy Spirit who gives you wisdom and direction. We are ready for battle, so it is time to move out with fresh anointing moving in the power of the almighty God. This is not the time to sit on the sideline and hold your heads down. This is the time to RISE UP and MOVE OUT! We have to stop running and start fighting. Warriors, it is time to get suited up and walk in your victory on a daily basis. Warriors, there is a sound and it is a sound calling you to battle. Warriors, can you hear the sound? This sound is awakening the warrior inside of you. It is calling you to come and join the other warriors on the battlefield.

Now look in the mirror again. What do you see? Are you beginning to see the warrior ready for battle? Are you beginning to see your spiritual muscles come out? After all of your training you should not see the same person that you saw in the beginning before your training. You should see a warrior that has grown in prayer, in fasting, in praise, in worship, and in the Word of God. Look closely. You should see the shift that has taken place. The Enemy can also see that you have changed. He can see that you are stronger than before. He can see that you have your full armor of God on and that you have a look on your face that means WAR! He knows that you are ready for battle, and he does not like it. But you are a relentless warrior who will not back down. You have a made up mind to complete the assignment the Commander- in-Chief has given you. Warriors, you are ready for battle. But as warriors for Christ we will not operate in manipulation towards upcoming warriors. We will not have a controlling spirit, nor a self-seeking spirit. We have committed to being honest and we shall love and not bully our fellow Soldiers. Although we are ready to battle we understand that we shall never come to a place where we think we can no longer train or learn anything new. My Pastor always tells us to remain FAT.....**F**aithful-**A**nd-**T**eachable. As warriors we must always remain faithful and teachable. We can never be in place as warriors that we do not remain teachable. When we get in that place we have just told God that we can no longer learn from Him because we know everything and that is a bad place to be. Warriors are continually pursuing spiritual growth in God. Warriors stand strong, because you stand in truth, we are not perfect but we are kingdom warriors who love the Lord and His word. Warriors you are ready for battle but understand in this battle we can never walk in unforgiveness. We have to walk in humility and not be angry with other warrior's positions. It is imperative that we stay delivered. Our strongest desire is to always be in God's presence. We do not want God to leave our presence because that is a dangerous place. We need God's presence everywhere we go. We need God's presence to push us forward. We need God's presence as Kingdom Warriors!

As warriors ready for battle we shall walk in cadence with our Commander-in-Chief. We will stay on beat, moving with Him at all times. Have you ever seen Soldiers march? They are all together marching on one accord, staying in step. That is how we need to be, staying in step with the Father's heartbeat. Staying in step with each other and not marching to our tune. It does not matter what it looks like; we will continue to stay on one accord on this battlefield. In the army there is a saying that goes, "it does not rain in the Army but on the

Army", meaning rain, problems, and situations do not stop the mission. Warriors, our motto should be, "God reigns on us and in our Army!" We serve a mighty God that reigns in our life. As warriors we have to let God reign in us and on us. We will not allow situations to reign over us. We shall continue the mission, and that is to tear down the Kingdom of Darkness. We are Warriors, ready for battle!

We are ready for battle, and we will never go AWOL (absent without leave), and we will never be AWOG (absent without God). We are warriors ready for battle. We don't quit; God didn't call us quitters. God called us "more than conquerors." We are Warriors ready for battle. We are committed to God; we have a made up mind to move forward and proceed with FORCE. Remember Warriors, you have been chosen! You were designed to be great! You were designed for this battle. Warrior, you were uniquely created. There is no other like you. You are an original. You are ready for battle. The warrior in you is ARISING! You will take your sword, and you will stand in position. You have accepted the call; you have accepted the responsibility. Warriors you are ready for battle!

As warriors ready for battle we shall continue to **RELEASE!** **R**unning-**E**very-**L**ap-**E**nduring-**A**ll-**S**ituations-**E**ncouraged! That is what we do, Warriors. We are runners, which is why we condition our bodies. As runners, we charge the Enemy and tear down his Kingdom of Darkness. We are in a race and shall complete this race that is set before us, which is why we are running every lap, every situation, every trail, everything that is trying to weigh us down. We are allowing God to turn them around to work in our favor. We are warriors who do not back down, but who RISE up against ALL situations. We don't let the Enemy frustrate us, but we know how to encourage ourselves in the midst of a situation. We are Warriors, and we are READY for BATTLE! We stand in a position of boldness, in a position of assurance because we know the God we serve is a strong and mighty God, who is a champion. And because He lives inside of us, we are MORE than conquerors. This fight is fixed; it is not even close because we are not fighting in our own strength. This is not just a regular victory; this win is by a landslide. And because you recognize who you are in Christ, you know that you are an overcomer. Warrior, you understand that while in this battle things may come your way that might try to shake you and devastate you, but because you are ready for battle nothing shall separate you from your God-given assignment. You are never alone in this battle, because God will never leave you nor forsake you. Warriors plant your feet and raise your BANNER of Victory! You are a Kingdom Warrior, and you are not backing down! GO FORTH and complete your assignment! GO FORTH and tear down the Kingdom of Darkness! Be strong and of good courage; do not be afraid nor be dismayed for the Lord our God is with you wherever you go. SO, GO FORTH in the Mighty, Matchless Name of Jesus!

Prayer

Father God, help me to continue to stand and fight in the battle. Help me to stay committed. I shall not give up, nor will I turn around. I am a warrior for life. I am a Kingdom warrior called to tear down the Kingdom of Darkness. I am Ready for Battle. Lord, thank You for making me a KINGDOM WARRIOR. Amen

IMPORTANT THINGS TO KEEP CLOSE

Kingdom Warrior Checklist

- ✓ Accepted the Calling -
- ✓ Understands the mission -
- ✓ Know and have a relationship with the Commander-in-Chief -
- ✓ Free from things that can hold you down -
- ✓ Fit to Fight –
- ✓ Armed with the weapon of Prayer –
- ✓ Loaded with arrows of Destruction –
- ✓ Fasted Life –
- ✓ Weapons of Praise –
- ✓ Dressed in the Full Armor of God –
- ✓ Secured in the Right Position -

Warriors remember to use your checklist each morning. Make sure you have a check by each item before you head out your door, because each one is needed. If any one area is lacking, make sure you go to God and get the fullness of what you need before you start your day. You are no longer in training, Warrior. You are a KINGDOM WARRIOR, READY FOR BATTLE!

Warrior Values

In the Army we had to live up to seven core values, and I believe it is also what God wants from His Kingdom Warriors.

Loyalty- A loyal warrior is one who supports his Commander-in-Chief, leaders, and stand up for fellow warriors. By wearing the full armor of God, we are expressing our loyalty, and we are expressing the loyalty we have to the Father.

Duty –Fulfill your obligations. Doing your duty means you are able to accomplish your tasks as part of a team. Your mission entails building one assignment to another. You fulfill your obligations as a part of your assignment every time you resist the Enemy, who wants you to take "short cuts" that might cause you to undermine or cause injury to your team.

Respect- Treat people as they should be treated. As a warrior for Christ, we should always treat our fellow warriors with dignity and respect, even if they do not show us the same gratitude. We are to always resemble Christ. We are made in His image so we should display His characteristics on a daily basis. When we respect others it allows us to appreciate the best in them. Remember we are one body with many different members, and all warriors have something to contribute. We should respect what they bring to the battlefield.

Selfless Service – Put the needs of the Lord above your own. Selfless service is bigger than you. In the Army of the Lord, you are doing what you are called to do without wanting to be recognized by man or to see your name in lights. You are committed to go a little further, endure a little longer, and push a little harder to make sure the mission is completed.

Honor – The highest honor a soldier in the military can get is The Medal of Honor. God wants to crown us with a Medal of Honor, Warrior. He wants us to make it a habit to live a lifestyle of respect, duty, loyalty, selfless service, and integrity. He wants us to honor Him with everything that we do. Give Honor to the Lord daily, Soldier.

Integrity- Always do what's right. As warriors, we are required not to say or do anything that will deceive others. Warrior, you should be a warrior of integrity so that others can trust the God in you. Your word and your actions should line up.

Personal Courage- Face fear, danger or adversity. As a warrior there may be times that you may have to stand alone and go the way God tells you to go. You might have to endure some rough terrains but - because you know that you serve a God that is mighty in battle and you know that He is with you all of the way - you will learn to encourage yourself and endure this battle.

Warriors Spiritual Tool Belt

Warriors, you have had your training, and you have on your whole armor of God and are ready for battle; but here is some more information for you to remember. Some may be a review of what of was taught earlier.

1. The **word of God...**If we are going to do anything we must have the word of God in us at all times. ***We cannot expect to be effective if we don't have the word of God in us.*** If we don't have our sword then we can't draw it and go to "war". The word of God explains who we are. How can we be warriors of God if we do not know who we are in God? The bible is basic instructions before leaving earth. The bible is our instruction manual for our lives. How can we know who we are and know how to operate ourselves if we don't take time out to read the manual on how we should function? When we war we have to be able to function even when we are frustrated. How can we know this if we don't take time to read the word of God and pray the word of God? The word of God helps us learn who we are and helps us on our daily journey in life. It teaches us about sin and what things to avoid that will put us in a pit. It teaches us patience instead of anger; it teaches us how to love instead of how to hate; it teaches us how to build people up instead of tearing people down and it teaches us humility. The word of God teaches me how to minister to people, how to treat people, how to be a mother, a spouse and a friend. It gives me lessons on how to minister comfort to those who

are hurting. But most importantly it teaches me how to minister to myself in this war. The word of God gives me direction in my life and in my ministry's life. If I am not following God and reading His word, how can I know which way is the right way to go? As Warriors, we need to make sure we are going in the right direction. So the word must be in us.

2. Prayer.... Prayer keeps us in constant communication with the Savior. We as warriors need to always seek the Father in prayer. ***Prayer is a must*** for kingdom warriors. Prayer produces faith. A warrior without a prayer life is like a skeleton less a body. A prayer life will lead us to conformation, conviction, revelation and declaration. Prayer will help us to stay firm in Jesus.

A prayer life will give us a boldness to stand for what is right. Without prayer you can war with your mind and knowledge, but the Holy Spirit will not be an active participant. Eventually whatever you are doing will lose its effectiveness because it is not God-directed. Prayer helps to order our steps. We are warring, but is our warring effective? It is only effective if we follow the lead of God through prayer and meditation. God cannot use us as kingdom warriors if we do not have a prayer life with Him. When we have a prayer life, it allows us to function under God's plans for our lives. Without prayer we will not understand the move of God's hand.

We must learn how to lay before God in prayer. Proskyneo (phonetic pronunciation: pros-koo-neh'-o). This is a position that you should always keep on your spiritual tool belt. Proskyneo is a Greek word that means, properly, to kiss the ground when prostrating before a superior; to *worship*, ready "to fall down/prostrate oneself to adore on one's knees". Worship is what I do but before I get up to worship, I must begin at the highest position, which is laying face down, worshiping the Father. I lay prostrate before the Father because I am giving Him reverence. I am worshipping Him; I am honoring the King of Kings. This position goes in sync with prayer. Laying before the Father is what we as Kingdom Warriors should do before we do anything else.

3. **Humility....** *But he giveth more grace. Wherefore he saith, God resisteth the proud, but giveth grace unto the humble.*

James 4:6

It is so important to keep humility on our spiritual belt because if we don't, we will fall into the trap of "we are doing this thing on our own", "we are the best warriors", and "church can't start until we arrive". We as warriors should not worry about our status, always hoping we get proper recognition for what we do. As Kingdom Warriors we should only worry about whether we are pleasing God. We must stay humble, and know that it is all God and give all the Glory to God. It's ok to say "thank you" when someone wants to say that you blessed them; but don't get into the habit and fall into the trap of pride because you start to think it's all you. Always remember we are only the willing vessel and God is working thru us. God can use anyone He chooses, and He choose us, so let us always remember to remain humble as we continue to tear down the Kingdom of Darkness.

4. **A Mentor...**It is very important to have a mentor on your tool belt. You need someone who can show you, help you, teach you and speak into your life. You have to make sure the mentor is someone God sent your way. For me, God will show me after I speak to a person a couple of times. I can remember one person I was speaking to. We never met before in person, and this was our very first conversation. We had spoken on the phone about dancing for about an hour and a half. And in that time of speaking, we both knew that it was a God connection. I learned so much on the phone with her in just that one conversation, and I knew I had to remain connected to her. I look forward to our conversations on the phone because she deposits things into my spirit and gives me a revelation. Now I can understand why I was doing this or why I was drawn to do this in the spirit. I am thankful God shows me things and tells me what to do, but I am even more grateful when He sends someone my way to give me a revelation on why I do what I do. Now I am in a position to teach others. So Warriors, make sure you seek the Lord on who should be mentoring you. You have to be very careful about who you let in to mentor you. Make sure you have heard from God and make sure what they are telling you is biblically based. If you do get a mentor, they should stretch you. The stretch may seem hard, but it is only preparing you for the next level.

5. **Basic First Aid Training...**Warriors in this war you will need to know basic first aid training to help you and your fellow warriors. You have to be alert and be able to recognize when your fellow warrior is wounded and needs assistance. You also need to be able recognize when you need assistance. In this war people can be damaged by getting offended, being malnourished from not getting their daily take of the word, and from being dehydrated. We all need to know **CPR**... We all need to know how to.........................

Cover....

Protect....

Reveal.....

We need to know how to **cover** our fellow warriors, when we see that they are tired and need to be restored. We have to learn to go to our fellow warrior and talk to them about what we see and give them a chance to get things right. We should never expose them and leave them for prey for the Enemy. We are family and we need to learn how to cover one another in this war. We have to learn to cover each other in prayer. Sometimes God may not want us to go to anyone because He just needs His warriors to cover people or situations in prayer. As we continue to cover things and people in prayer, God will continue to **protect** them. God is our shield and our buckler. He is our mighty protector, and as we are in His arms of comfort and safety, He will begin to reveal things to us about what is going on.

He will reveal His plan for our lives. He will **reveal** mysteries to His warriors. And once God reveals to you, He will put you in a position to reveal to His people. So we need to make sure we are aware of how to conduct CPR. Cover...Protect...Reveal. During CPR God can breathe the fresh breath of heaven back into us to revive us and recharge us. As warriors we need to be recharged and revived. We can never keep going forward and not taking the time to get recharged by God.

These are just the basic things you need on your spiritual tool belt, but as you grow and seek His face, He will show you other things that are needed. Stay in tune so you can hear Him.

Discussion/Self Check

1. Why do you think prayer is important to have on your spiritual tool belt? ____________________

____

____

____

2. Why do you think it is important to have a mentor?

____

____

3. Why do you think CPR is important? __________

____

____

4. Do you see yourself missing any of the spiritual tools on your tool belt?

____

____

Commander In-Chief Names to Call On!

Jehovah Tsaba – ***The Lord our Warrior***

1 Sam 17:45 - *Then said David to the Philistine, Thou comest to me with a sword, and with a spear, and with a shield: but I come to thee in the name of the LORD of hosts, the God of the armies of Israel, whom thou hast defied.*

In this battle, you have to know who to call on. You have to know that satan is a lot of things, but our Lord is OUR WARRIOR. God is the ALMIGHTY WARRIOR and the Lion of Judah. When we call on Jehovah Tsaba we are calling on the Lord our Warrior. He WARS on our behalf. He is the MIGHTY WARRIOR; that is why HE is our Trainer

Jehovah El Nose – ***The Forgiving God***

Psalm 99:8 – *Thou answeredst them, O LORD our GOD: thou wast a God that forgavest them, though thou tookest vengeance of their inventions.*

Warrior, no matter what you have done, God is a forgiving God. Repent and turn from your old ways. You have enlisted in the Lord's Army so do not let your past be a hindrance to you moving forward in this battle. Call on Jehovah El Nose, He is the Forgiving God.

<u>Jehovah Ezer</u> – *The Lord is our Helper*

Hebrews 13:6 – *So that we may boldly say, The Lord is my helper, and I will not fear what man shall do unto me.*

Remember the Lord is always your helper warrior. It does not matter what man may say or try to do. We shall not fear, because we have the Great Helper in this spiritual battle.

<u>Jehovah El Roi</u> – *The God who Sees*

Genesis 16:13 – *And she called the name of the Lord that spake unto her, Thou God seest me: for she said, Have I also here looked after him that seeth me?*

Warrior, God sees ALL. He sees you when you are feeling lonely. He sees you when you are feeling defeated. He sees you and because He sees and He loves you, He takes care of you. He sees you through the battle. He sees you through the pain and the hurt. So remember next time you are on the battle field and you feel lonely, remember to call on the name Jehovah El Roi, the God who Sees.

Jehovah Gibbor Milchamah – ***The Lord Mighty in Battle***

Psalm 24:8 – *Who is the King of Glory? The Lord strong and mighty, the Lord mighty in battle.*

The Lord our God whom we serve is strong and mighty in battle. There is not any battle that HE is not stronger than. If you are battling in your body, in your marriage, in your finances or whatever your battle may be warrior, our God is stronger than that. You do not have to feel like you are sinking, call our Jehovah Gibbor Milchamah, HE is STRONG in every one of your BATTLES!

Jehovah Chereb – ***The Glorious Sword of the Lord***

Deuteronomy 33:29 – *Happy art thou, O Israel: who is like unto thee, O people saved by the Lord, the shield of they help, and who is the sword of thy excellency! and thine enemies shall be found liars unto thee; and thou shalt tread upon their high places.*

Warrior, you have assured victory because Jehovah Chereb is the glorious sword of the Lord. Nothing is able to prevail against Him. So when you feel like you do not have the victory call on the name Jehovah Chereb and be rest assured that His Glorious Sword is fighting ALL battles in our lives.

Elohei Ma'uzzi – God of my Strength

Psalm 43:2 – *For thou art the God of my strength: why dost thou cast me off? why go I mourning because of the oppression of the enemy?*

Warrior, in this war, you have to remind yourself that He is the God of your Strength. There will be challenges that you are faced with in this war and it will feel like everything is stacked up against you and it feels like you are sinking. But this is the time to call on Elohei Ma'uzzi, the God of your Strength! Stop relying on your own strength, Warrior. Call on Elohei Ma'uzzi.

READY FOR BATTLE!

ENCOURAGING WORDS!

Warriors, the time has come. I pray that this training has equipped you and will launch you to be the warrior that God has called you to be. Always remember Warrior, in order to tear down the Kingdom of Darkness, you must prepare for battle, and equipped yourself for battle. Remember these basic steps will prepare you for any battle that you might come up against. It is time for you to ARISE, ACCEPT THE CALL and MOVE FORWARD. This is the season in which God is calling all warriors to get trained, so that they are ready for their assignment from Him. So Warrior, I say to you, **"BE BRAVE, BE BOLD, and BE BLESSED!"**

BE BRAVE.....the battle is already won. God did not give you the spirit of fear! Hold your head up high and GO FORTH Kingdom Warrior!

BE BOLD.....GO FORTH in boldness because you know who goes before you and you know who is with you! The GREAT I AM is with you during the battle every single day!

BE BLESSED.....be blessed Kingdom Warrior. You are blessed because you are a child of the Most High. You are blessed because you said, "YES." You are blessed because God says you are blessed in the field, you are blessed in the city, you are blessed when you are coming, you are blessed when you leave and you are blessed in the BATTLE!!

READY FOR BATTLE!

ABOUT THE AUTHOR!

Dr. Wanda Cofield, is a wife, Mother and a licensed Ordained Elder, who holds a Doctoral degree in Pastoral Care. God has called her to birth the ministry Prophetically Spoken Ministries, where the word of God is brought prophetically through dancing, preaching and teaching. Her ministry's heart and mission is setting the captives free to walk in the boldness to which God has called them to without fear or doubt.

If you are looking for strongholds to be broken; prophetic workshops, dance workshops, ministry in word or dance, please contact:

Dr. Wanda Cofield
Number: 404-946-8171

Website Address:
www.propheticallyspokenministries.com

Email Address:
Kingdomwarrior03@gmail.com

Made in the USA
Columbia, SC
12 October 2021

46679049R00075